The Memory Stays

The Memory Stays

(And in such detail)

Alexander Pullar

To order additional copies of this book, contact:
Xlibris
UK TFN: 0800 0148620 (Toll Free inside the UK)
UK Local: 02036 956328 (+44 20 3695 6328 from outside the UK)
www.Xlibrispublishing.co.uk
Orders@Xlibrispublishing.co.uk
774356

CONTENTS

Preface

My mother, Bessie Pullar (1903–2000), outlived most of her early peers. However, she kept alive the memory of bygone generations by clearly recalling their names and stories and explaining how they fitted into her own family life. She was an enthusiastic storyteller, and many of these stories she wrote down, dedicating them all to her late husband (Sandy), her two sons, and her six grandchildren.

I in turn have dedicated this book to my parents' memory and to all those who were in some way part of their lives; they have all contributed to its writing. It contains many of the stories told to me by my parents and grandparents. Hence, this book is largely a biographical account of my family's history in the city of Dundee.

Something about the Author

Frequently, I have changed direction in life, often for the sole purpose of acquiring a greater knowledge and experience of something new. However, since my primary school days and the influence of my elder brother, who was eleven years my senior, I have always been fascinated with the ancient city of Rome and its astonishing history. This led to my complete captivation and study of ancient history and archaic myths. It was therefore quite surprising that in later life I emerged from university with a BSc degree, and in so doing, I started a teaching career in mathematics.

This was not quite what I wanted or was meant to do; however, it had become my livelihood. In time, with a diploma in computing, I took control of the school's embryonic computer department and apparently drifted even further from my true purpose in life. My next step was to leave the school system and enter the world of further education as a computing lecturer, which was more suited to my lifestyle and proved to be a far more satisfying and rewarding career. This shift in occupation, in effect, gave me more time, which I put to good use, eventually gaining a BA degree from the Open University.

With my family now starting to follow their own careers and seek their own journeys into life, I knew that my lifecycle had not yet come to an end and that I had more to offer. This new BA degree was therefore the marker whereby I could restart my obsession with the long-gone days of the past. Now was the time to vivaciously rekindle my interest in ancient history and the city of Rome. So after some ten years in the world of computing, I retired early. However, I did continue as a part-time supply teacher in the local schools and colleges, and on occasions I lectured on archaic and ancient history in the Department of Continuous Education at Dundee University. Love of the ancients and my infatuation with the Eternal City quickly led to countless visits and stays, absorbing more of the city's past with each visit. Eventually, my enthusiasm led to organising and conducting exclusive guided tours to Rome; it also led to the writing of my first book, *Dust of Gods*. These experiences have become among the most satisfying and successful highlights in my life.

Encouraged by my partner, Elizabeth Henderson, I concentrated on and became preoccupied with the history of both sides of my family (the Pullars and the McElroys). I also became fascinated in the old and recent history of my own hometown, Dundee. This provided the platform whereby I wrote a biography of my parents' respective family trees and how they fitted into the history of their home city, enabling them to take their proper place in Dundee's past.

Preview

With the passing of time, family history can become a vague distant memory disconnected to present-day affairs. If passed by word of mouth through the generations, family matters will ultimately erode and disappear or, at best, become blurred in favour of the current and no doubt biased exposé of the tale. Hence, the true past will fade into obscurity and be lost forever. This book is an attempt to preserve the authentic history of two Dundee families through the nineteenth and twentieth centuries—the "Pullars of the Hilltown" and the McElroys of Dallfield Walk—preventing their loss to the abrasive passage of time.

However, this is not simply a glimpse into their everyday lives. It is set against a background of local, national, and international affairs and is an attempt to clarify the significant effects of such events on the lives of simple working people. Not only is it a biography of both my parents and their respective families, but it reflects the consequences of such events that many similar poverty-afflicted families had to endure during a period of Britain's supreme industrial might and prosperity.

Therefore, it echoes a bygone age in the history of this ancient city, which tells of a time when life was hard and often short. But it also tells of an age when people had time for each other, time to stop, time to speak, and time to listen.

CHAPTER 1

A Quick Look at Bygone Days

Prehistory

This is not an attempt to give an in-depth history of the city. Nor will I provide an extensive list of eminent people who were born within its boundaries or had an association with it. Nevertheless, there are some outstanding historical events and renowned individuals who will always be associated with ancient Dundee; it would therefore be to my utter neglect as an author if I were to omit their mention.

This ancient Scottish burgh is situated on the northern shore of an ancient river system that empties into the North Sea, the River Tay. The river originally carved its way through a series of fault lines that run along the axis of a geological anticline, of which the Angus-Perthshire Sidlaw Hills and the Lomond Range in Fife are the remnant stumps. Also, Scotland's rainfall is mainly carried inland on a prevailing westerly wind flow, whereby most of the country's wet weather is largely offloaded over its western summits. This leaves the east coast relatively dry, hence the expression "Sunny Dundee."

It is principally to this river, the longest in Scotland, with its wide tidal estuary and deep-water harbour, that Dundee owes its existence. The seasonal temperature of the water at the estuary varies by an average of only one degree Celsius and results in the adjacent lands enjoying a mild climate, in relative contrast to that farther inland.

The name of the city was probably from Gaelic-Pictish origins: "dun" meaning "fort" and "dee" from the Gaelic "Dèagh" meaning "fire." The name of the river was initially recorded as "Taoua" in the mid first century AD, by Claudius Ptolemaeus. He lived in Alexandria, Egypt, and was a Graeco-Roman man of science who had an interest in astronomy and geography. In modern Gaelic, it was referred to as "Uisge Tatha," meaning "Water of the Tay."

Dundee flanks the northern bank of the Tay estuary. The city is dominated by two distinctive hills, respectively known as the Law, or more correctly, the Dundee Law (175 m), and its lesser companion, the Hill of Balgay (134 m). These hills were wrongly regarded as substantial and active archaic volcanoes, 400 million years old, which eroded apparently into volcanic plugs as seen today. But recent research has shown that this is not the case; instead, they are part of an intrusive sill of solidified andesite magma, which has squeezed through fishers (or cracks) in the bedrock, and by erosion of the surrounding country, they have taken up their plug-like formations. This type of rock is the product of two colliding geological plates, one of which is subducted below the other and swallowed into the mantle of the earth. This occurs along a fracture line known as the Benioff Sheer Zone, and the process alters the subducted rock into a magma type known as andesite. This new andesitic magma can return to the surface through a series of fissures or volcanoes that could form great expanses of igneous lava flows. Weathering and erosion then take over, often producing a rough hilly terrain of great lava-flow mounds stretching for miles over the adjacent areas. Clepington Road in the north of the city is one such flow.

With the onset of the last ice age, the movement of a glacier from west to east along the Tay Valley further eroded the volcanic landscape; the Dundee Law took the shape of a crag and tail feature; the crag is the steep eroded side of the plug, part of which is now Dundee's Campbell Street, and on the opposite side, the tail where the eroded material was redeposited and is now the city's Hilltown district. It was upon this extreme terrain that Dundee was built, which makes it one of the hilliest cities in the country.

The summit of the Dundee Law was levelled almost flat by Pictish tribes; they were the incumbents who occupied the northern regions of Scotland in ancient times. From the residue of the rock that remained of their labour, they built a substantial Iron Age hill fort that was formidable enough to deter an enemy and provide refuge for the local inhabitants and their livestock during times of siege. This fortified hill was striking enough to be clearly marked on the primitive maps of the frequent marauding bands of invading Vikings, who referred to it simply as the "Law"—an ancient Scottish word meaning "hill." In present-day Dundee vernacular, it is often referred to as the "Law Hill," which literally means "Hill Hill." It was here that Viscount Dundee, on 13 April 1689, initially raised the royal standard of the Stuarts, marking the start of the First Jacobite Rising.

To the east of the Law stands the second volcanic mound, Balgay Hill, which derived its name from the Gaelic meaning "stead of the marsh/wind." It is not as high as its more celebrated neighbour but is prominent enough to be part of the famous silhouetted profile of the city, especially when set against the stunning easterly sunsets over the river.

On Balgay's summit sits Mills Observatory, the first full-time publicly owned observatory in the country. During part of my youth, this observatory acted as my second home. This was where my brother Bill and I would observe the heavenly bodies of the winter night sky, often in zero-degree temperature. On the way home after a few hours of this ice-cold experience, Bill, who is my senior by some ten years, would buy me a welcome bag of hot steaming chips. He was by far the most studious in the family and was constantly seen with a book in his hand. Not surprisingly, he became a proof-reader with the local newspaper, *D C Thomson*, and later, in his late twenties, he entered Dundee University, going on to become a teacher of geography.

In prehistoric times, most of Caledonia (Scotland, or Alba in Gaelic) was hidden in a thick blanket of woodland occupied by various predators, the most prolific of which was the first indigenous humans to occupy the northern region of the country, the scantily clad Picts. As the last great ice sheet retreated some 12,000 years ago, they followed this retreat from Scandinavia, settling in the Orkney Islands before crossing onto the mainland. Their presence is still evidenced today by the famous prehistoric structures of Skara Brae, Maeshowe, and the Rings of Brodgar. This was followed by a steady flow of Gaelic-speaking Irish who settled in the west of the country. Eventually, these Irish settlers, or Scots, amalgamated with the Picts, who adopted their language.

The first inhabitants of north Tayside lived during the Mesolithic era (circa 8000 BC), and in early Pictish times, it was part of the Kingdom of Circinn, which occupied an area like that of the present county of Angus. To the south lay another domain of the Picts, the Kingdom of Fib (now Fife).

The first battle to be fought in the Dundee area was the Battle of Pitalpin, not far from the village of Liff. It was fought between King Alpin (for the Scots) and King Brude (of the Picts). Alpin was defeated and attempted to escape. The track he followed was to the north of present Dundee towards the coast. It is the same route now followed by Dundee's bypass, which has been appropriately named "Kingsway."

King Alpin was captured, and his headless body was cast into a pit (or grave), hence the name "Pitalpin." The head was then carried off by the victorious Picts. In time, there was the inevitable alliance between the two belligerent nations, coming together under the House of Alpin to create Alba, which is the Gaelic name for Scotland. In translation, it means "Scotland forever."

By the time Rome attempted to subdue the Picts (circa AD 82), about half of the woodlands that had covered Scotland were gone due to the increasing activities of man. From the Neolithic times, this was the case along the flat region of the Tay Valley, where the mineral-rich volcanic soil provided great expanses of fertile land suitable for settlement. So in the shadow of their fortified hill, the original native community stretched far along the valley's flat alluvium plain to the Carse of Gowrie, through which the freshwater Tay meandered. The population consisted of hunter-gatherers, farmers, and towards the saltwater estuary, fishermen who hunted the intertidal zone for rich seafood. Archaeologists have found rubbish pits (middens) containing seashells and fish remains dating as far back as the late Bronze Age (800 BC for Scotland). These original hunter-gatherers probably interacted and traded with other local tribes; eventually, trade routes spread far beyond this riverside region. Hence, with a plentiful supply of food, extensive trade routes, and a hill fort for defence, this locality became a sheltered haven, which has been continually inhabited since prehistoric times. Even with the arrival of a Roman army and fleet, which anchored in the mouth of the Tay, life continued as normal.

The Romans set up a series of camps and signal stations to keep an eye on the wild Pict tribes that would regularly appear out from the northern glens, ravaging and pillaging as they went. The remains of one such Roman camp has been located close to the village of Longforgan, some five miles to the east of the Dundee Law, and is in direct line of sight of a Roman signal station that had been located on the hill's summit. A Roman fleet supplied the army, which was led by the governor, Agricola, in his attempt to conquer the whole of this triangular island of Britannia. The combined tribes of Picts from the north, under their leader Calgacus, met the Romans at a place called Mons Graupius, to the east of present-day Inverness. The Picts were defeated in an open-pitched battle, but eventually they won the war as Rome never quite conquered north Britain (Alba).

CHAPTER 2

A Struggling Scotland

Sir William Wallace

Dundee has a history that is dotted with colour, and one such colourful event occurred in the year 1291. A young man by the name of William Wallace was sent to Dundee to round off his formal education, and for a while he studied at the Dundee High School. At that time, Dundee was occupied by English forces, and regrettably Wallace had the misfortune of ending his conventional schooling by stabbing to death the incumbent governor's son. Now a renegade, Wallace found it necessary to flee the city, which he did with great haste; this was his first blow for Scotland in its struggle for independence from England. However, the only visual evidence that the city fathers could muster in commemoration of such a momentous episode in Scottish history was a small communal plaque attached to the wall of St Paul's Cathedral in the city centre. Hardly a fitting marker for such an important man or event. This was of such historical significance in the history of Dundee that its citizens should always hold their heads high with pride; it led directly to Scotland's independence.

William Wallace's plaque, attached to the wall of St Paul's
Cathedral, Dundee (shared with Admiral Duncan).

English Influence

Great suspicion existed between Scotland and England due to the
Scottish alliance with France (the Auld Alliance of 1295). However,
there was an attempt to cement over such differences with a proposed
marriage between Mary, Queen of Scots, and Edward (son of Henry
VIII), but this was doomed to failure, resulting in the invasion of
Scotland by its southern neighbour. This was referred to as the
"Rough Whooing," and Dundee was in the forefront.

In 1544, Dundee's population was stricken by plague; these poor
victims were set outside the East Gate (or the Wishart Arch), where
they were preached to by the Protestant leader George Wishart. This
meant that Dundee was in no fit state to defend itself and quickly fell
to an English army, led by Andrew Dudley, who along with his fleet,
had taken Broughty Castle, in 1547. Dundee was sacked and suffered
greatly from plunder and pillage, which continued throughout the
region. In that same year, Balmerino Abbey in Fife was torched by

7

these English invaders; thereafter, both city and abbey lay in ruins for many years.

Meanwhile, Mary, Queen of Scots, had been betrothed to the Dauphin of France (later to be Francois II), removing any prospects of a marriage between her and Edward. This was an important union with the French despite the financial cost of the wedding to this small and relatively poor nation. The estimated cost was in the region of £10,000 and was met by donations from the respective burghs throughout the land; Dundee's share was around £1200, making it the second largest contributor, second only to Edinburgh. However, it also meant that Francois, upon his marriage to Mary, would become king consort of Scotland. This was a perilous situation for the Scots as, having removed an English threat of annexation, they were now faced with a similar menace from the French. Reinforcing such a marriage was Mary's mother, Mary of Guise, the French-born wife of James V. She was regent to Scotland from 1554 to 1560 and wished her adopted country to be Catholic.

However, with the signing of the Treaty of Norham in 1551, things became more settled between Scotland and its neighbour to the south. At least for a while, peace existed throughout this troubled land, but it was not a lasting peace. Over the horizon loomed yet more trouble for the Scots as they were plunged into two more decades of disordered turmoil.

The year after the Treaty of Norham, Mary, Queen of Scots, who was a staunch Catholic, was widowed. She returned to her native country and almost immediately old religious divisions were brought to the surface. In 1559, the abbeys of Balmerino, Scone, and Lindores were destroyed by reformers, mainly from Dundee. This was civil war, and the unrest continued until Mary's defeat at the Battle of Langside (1568), followed by her detention via the order of England's Queen Elizabeth, ultimately leading to Mary's execution. By then, Scotland was a Protestant nation—in name only.

Sack of Dundee (General Monck)

Dundee, having learnt its lesson after its sack by Andrew Dudley's army, rebuilt an even stronger defensive wall round the burgh. It was now regarded as a safe and secure place, so much so that even the capital deposited much of its gold reserves in the Dundee vaults. However, gunpowder had become a feature of warfare over the one hundred years that had elapsed between the erection of this defensive wall of stone and the appearance of General Monck in 1651.

Monck was one of Cromwell's best republican generals who had been sent north to quell the Scots. Dundonians had remained loyal to the crown during the Civil War (1642–1651) and were staunch supporters of Charles II. They also held a great deal of the country's wealth. Hence, it was a prime target for the 7,000-strong Puritan force that arrived at its gates in August 1651. Despite the strong ring of stone defending the city, this was no match against cannon fire; also, demon drink played its part in the city's downfall.

Point where Monck's cannon ball struck St Mary's Steeple.

Once the siege had started, the semi-inebriated garrison took only half an hour to be overpowered. The result was a great slaughter of its citizens and was one of the worst accounts of butchery and carnage in Scottish history. Five thousand Dundee citizens were murdered, and many women were raped; today these atrocities would have been regarded as war crimes, but Monck got away with it. The objective of the sack was the theft of the vast fortune held in the burgh's treasury, which fell into the hands of General Monck. The fortune in the vaults alone amounted to some £2.5 million, including Monck's prize money, but in addition to this thievery were the valuables stolen from the private citizens. This left them and the city ruined. This plunder, which included vast amounts of jewellery, coinage, and pickings of gold and silver, were loaded onto sixty commandeered ships. They then set sail from Dundee harbour on their journey south, presumably first to Leith then on to England.

However, this was not to be, as if in retaliation for this vile act of wickedness, the wrath of God struck. A September storm with gale-force winds blew down the length of the Tay Valley. Monck's sixty-strong fleet was caught with their sails up at the mouth of the river, where they were pounded by mountainous waves and strong winds. This wrecked and sank the entire fleet, whereby their precious cargo was completely lost. (To this day, nothing has been recovered.) But Monck managed to survive. Later, after the death of Cromwell, this professional soldier cannily switched sides, becoming a staunch Royalist. Eventually, with great pomp and ceremony, and much honour, this man was buried in Westminster Abbey. So much for Dundee's loyal sacrifice to the crown.

Of course, there were many more battles to be fought on Scottish soil during the next one hundred years, including the Jacobite Rebellion of 1689, during which was fought the Battle of Killiecrankie (involving the famous Soldier's Leap). Also, the second Jacobite Rebellion of 1745, which put an end to the Royal Stuarts' attempt to reclaim the throne. Culmination finally came with the Jacobite defeat at Culloden in 1746. The Battle of Culloden was the last to be fought on British soil and saw an end to sackings and revolution. Burgh defences were no longer an essential part of life, and the defensive wall that once ringed Dundee was dismantled, except for the East Port (or Wishart Arch). This was kept for posterity and in memory of George Wishart, who preached and ungrudgingly tended to the plague victims of the burgh.

Wishart Arch, Dundee.

CHAPTER 3

Women of Dundee

Frances Wright

A Dundee aristocratic woman, by the name of Frances (Fanny) Wright, was born in 1795. The family was successful in the manufacture of linen, but she was orphaned early in life and went to live with her grandfather in London. Frances, as a wealthy woman, eventually settled in the United States of America, where she was appalled at the atrocious treatment of African slaves. Frances spent the rest of her life fighting against the inhumanity of the transatlantic slave trade, whereby millions of captured Africans were shipped to the Americas in British ships. Abolition of the slave trade occurred in 1807, but it took until 1833 for slavery to be abolished throughout the British Empire. Nevertheless, it continued illegally for many decades after that, despite compensation paid to the slave owners, which in total reached the staggering sum of £20 million. Much of this money, however, was used to reinvest in the slave plantations of America. In the southern United States, according to the census of 1860, there were almost 4 million slaves.

Frances Wright died in Ohio in 1852, never having seen the abolition of slavery throughout the United States, which was ended by the American Civil War (1861—1865).

Mary Shelley

During the early part of the nineteenth century, to be exact, 1812, a sprightly but ailing young schoolgirl by the name of Mary Wollstonesraft Godwin came to the city under the protection of the Baxter family, which was one of the famous jute baron families of Dundee; they owned a large mansion (Ellen Gowan) just to the east of the city. Close by, Mary spent some two years of her young, impressionable life housed in a cottage close to present-day South Baffin Street, from where she enhanced her vivid imagination with the coarse harshness of an environment she had never experienced. Coupled with her assertive nature, she undoubtedly met with local workers from her host's mills and was aware of their plight. Stricken with poverty, starvation, disease, and a high child mortality, these people so impressed her innocent mind that from the plummeted depth of despaired memories, Mary Shelley produced the character of Frankenstein.

Mary Slessor

Mary Shelley certainly saw, but did not experience, the hardship suffered by these workers, but there was another Mary, who did. Again connected to the Baxter family, but decades later, and by no means a house guest, Mary Mitchell Slessor worked as a lowly weaver. She was not only aware of the deprivation that existed but was part of the 90,000 jute workers who were occupying the city's mills and factories.

Born in Aberdeen in 1848, her family made the short journey to Dundee, when she was aged 10 years, to find a new life. But with an alcoholic father, they found themselves living in abject poverty. With such experiences, Mary appeared to have little chance of achieving her goal of missionary work in Africa, which appeared to be the sole prerogative of the richer classes. However, having received a rudimentary education provided by the Baxter brothers, she continued her education and was finally trained by the Presbyterian Church of Scotland as a teacher in Edinburgh. At the age of 28, she left for Calabar, in the south of Nigeria. There, as a missionary, she worked and lived with the Okiyong tribes, learning their language (Efic) and their superstitions, one of which involved the abandonment of newly born twins to die in the bush. They believed that an evil spirit possessed one of the babies and, not knowing which one, rejected both. By saving these abandoned children, she often brought them up as her own.

From a particularly bad attack of malaria, an infection that had periodically dogged her since she first arrived in Nigeria, this revered and honoured Scottish lady died on 13 January 1915 at the age of 66.

CHAPTER 4

Fortune and Fate

Dundee's Whaling Past

D undee by the nineteenth century was open for business, and one of the first industries to take advantage of the city's location, its harbour facilities, and the potential of its population was whaling. In fact, whaling had existed from the mid seventeenth century and continued through until the early twentieth. But its zenith as a whaling centre, the largest of its kind in Northern Europe, started and continued all during the nineteenth century.

Nevertheless, it is now difficult to find any legacy of Dundee's whaling past, apart from a few old retained street names, which are poignant reminder of those forgotten days: Baffin Street, named after Canada's Baffin Island, and East and West Whale Lanes, the very streets along which the carcases of these gigantic mammals were hauled. These great beasts were then dissected, and their precious mineral rich blubber was boiled down into whale oil used for countless beneficial purposes, including oil lamp lighting, medicine, and soaps. None of the whale carcass were discarded; even the whalebone was used for lady's corsets, and their skin for aesthetic decoration.

By the early nineteenth century, Dundee had already established a linen industry, probably due to the fast streams flowing down its steep slopes, thus providing the energy to turn the mill wheels. Such regions became large and important centres for the manufacture of linen. However, if it had not been for the presence of the whaling industry in Dundee, the city's progress into the nineteenth century may have been completely different. Along with the advent of steam-powered looms, there was what could only be described as a revelation to the city's textile industry. The successful treatment of raw jute yarn with whale oil in the 1830s produced a low-priced yarn that was strong, pliable, and resistant to breaking. The jute textile industry had been born, and it dominated Dundee's way of life for the next century.

King Jute

Jute is a plant that is mainly grown in the hot humid climate of Bangladesh (East Bengal). It grows to a maximum height of fifteen feet and produces a fibre that is ideal for coarse products, including carpet backing, sacks, and canvas. It was around the 1840s that jute was beginning to have a significant effect on the Dundee textile industry. The population of this burgh grew from a mere 4,000 in 1831 to 55,000 a decade later. And with the introduction of pure jute cloth, it overtook linen in the 1850s, when David Taylor was granted the first jute patent in 1852 (Thomson, Shepherd & Co. Ltd, Seafield Works, Taylor's Lane). Nevertheless, the burgh had not significantly expanded, mainly due to geological restrictions, so accommodation for this large influx of people ultimately resulted in an acute housing shortage and extreme overcrowding.

Although the first imported consignments had appeared in 1822, the transition to jute was not easy, and as late as 1839, this new fibre was still being described by the *Dundee Advertiser* as "rubbish." Nevertheless, with the onset of the American Civil War and the resulting disruption to cotton supplies, jute became the preferred and permanent fibre.

This durable new product transformed the city into the prosperous industrial jute centre of the world; jute had become the world's leading hard-wearing durable natural fibre, which easily degenerated back into the environment. It was used in the manufacture of countless products, including ship's sails, a commodity which was eagerly taken up by both the whaling industry and the Royal Navy; the navy was one of the main customers. Along with the supply of sail fabric, there were numerous other products, including canvas bags (used for sandbags particularly during times of war) and high-quality carpets. Almost every household in the city possessed such a carpet, which had been obtained under somewhat dubious circumstances. Jute even covered the waggons during the advance of the American settlers over the prairies of the Wild West. All products of the Dundee worker.

The jute plant was transported in raw bails by large, oceangoing ships to the deepwater harbour of Dundee. By now, Jute had overtaken whaling as Dundee's main industry, despite the fleet possessing ten steam-powered vessels by 1873. With an unlimited supply of whale oil and ideally situated for both the European and American markets, the city depended and thrived on the manufacture and distribution of its jute products for almost one hundred years. It was little wonder that it had rightfully acquired the title King Jute.

Although the city's population stood at over 64,000, according to the 1851 survey, Dundee had still not expanded due to the steep topography that surrounded it. By the mid nineteenth century, north-running streets had been blasted through from the old city centre to the cotton and jute developments to the north. Castle Street, opened in 1785, had been excavated through a black igneous intrusion of dolerite rock that had extended out into the River Tay. Upon this outcrop once stood the Dundee Castle, which dated back to the twelfth century when Dundee was made a Royal burgh. Another new line of communication that ran north from the harbour was Union Street, created in the mid nineteenth century. These streets allowed Dundee to fully participate in the developing textile industry. This expansion from the ancient centre followed the original river and stream systems, including the Scouring and Dens Burns. Extending into the county of Angus, these textile industries could be found as far north in the villages of Coupar Angus, Forfar, and Blairgowrie.

The Jute Barons

Jute was king, and the king was David Baxter, the first of the jute barons, who along with his new partner, a talented engineer called Peter Carmichael, made the city of Dundee one of the largest manufacturing centres in the world.

Of course, there were other jute barons who, like the Baxter family, had become extremely rich. One notable person was James K Caird; he expanded the family business in the latter half of the nineteenth century. He was continuing his father's work of producing cloth entirely made from jute fibre. Between the years 1905 and 1925, James Caird, and his sister, Mrs Grace Marryatt, contributed around a quarter of a million pounds to the city. This was by way of leisure parks (Caird Park, the Den of Mains, and a golf course) and the massively impressive Caird Hall, which now dominates the centre of the city.

Another pioneer in the field of powered looms and the sole user of jute was James Cox. By 1841 this had become a family concern when a partnership was formed with three of his brothers, and under the name of Cox Bros Ltd, it quickly expanded. The year 1848 saw one of the largest factory complexes to be built in Europe, the Camperdown Works, close to the village of Lochee. It had been consumed into the burgh of Dundee around 1833 and lay to the north-west of the city. This manufacturing complex was connected directly to the harbour and dockland area of the city by the latest of innovations, a steam-powered rail link. The Cox family also lavished a great deal of time and money on an overall grandiose factory design which that the style of the Italian Renaissance. In 1866 this included an eighty-five-metre (282 feet) high chimney stalk in the style of an Italian campanile. Yet again, the jute workers were endowed with another leisure park, this time the twenty-five-acre Lochee Park adjacent to Balgay Hill.

I am sure that the weavers, winders, twisters, spinners, baggers, tenters, and rest of the workforce employed by these jute entrepreneurs appreciated the lavish gifts bestowed upon them from their employers. However, working from six in the morning till six at night, with only a half day on Saturday, followed by an expected double attendance at church or chapel on Sunday, left little time for a leisurely stroll through these parks, perhaps with a library book (or Bible) tucked under one's arm. It was the job of the woman, who made up most of the workforce, to return home from a day's work in a Dundee jute mill, one of the hardest, most sweat-drenched jobs on the planet, only to start toiling at home cleaning, washing, feeding, and generally bringing up the family. I am quite sure that working people would have appreciated, more so than a park, an adequate and subsidised water supply, which was not forthcoming until 1876. On occasions it was suggested that the Dundonian, in the mid nineteenth century, was not convinced of the need for simple hygiene. If the jute barons had spent a little more time enlightening their workers and concentrated on adequate housing and basic amenities, then survival rates may have been improved among these deprived employees.

A Precarious Water Supply

Up until then, public and industrial supplies of water depended largely on local wells, which included the Hilltown's Lady Well. This was originally called the Well of the Blessed Marie de Dundee. (During medieval times, it had been known as the Holy Well.) In 1777, a well formally situated at Tendall's Wynd was moved to behind the Old Town House. This was St Clement's Well, but in 1872, it was permanently removed. To distribute the water throughout the city, it was normal practice for carts, each loaded with 1,000-gallon water tanks, to be used. This supply was mainly from Lochee's Smellies Well, but when required, carts from Invergowrie (a village to the west) and Newport in Fife helped supply the city.

The cholera pandemic that had spread worldwide between 1829 and 1851 had arrived in Dundee by 1832. It was a disease susceptible only to humans and spread mainly through faeces-contaminated water, to which this burgh was predisposed; the lack of wholesome food was a secondary factor. The whole burgh was stricken by the outbreak, which was referred to as the "fever." A daily toll of deaths was posted on the walls of the Pillars townhouse each day. In total, out of a population of around 30,000 inhabitants, there were recorded in excess of five hundred who died from this contagious disease.

There were so many corpses that a trench was opened in the Howff burial ground; there, dignified with individual coffins, their bodies still lie in a mass grave. The only marker left is that of a single headstone to William Forrest Esquire, 1832.

However, there were other diseases that continually scourged the city's population, particularly typhoid, tuberculosis, smallpox, and measles. They periodically ravaged the burgh until the Public Health Act 1875, which was significant in the alleviation of these problems.

Headstone of William Forrest Esquire in
the Howff Cemetery, Dundee.

Of course, this had little effect on the mill owners; they simply moved out to their country seats. These employers were all millionaires (billionaires by today's standards) who lived only within a few miles distance of the vermin-infested tenements they had so kindly built and rented out to their employees. They obviously knew about the unwholesome circumstances under which their workers were expected to live but had become all too conditioned in the art of turning a blind eye. I can only imagine the pleading, corruption, and abuse that families had to suffer in their desperate scramble to place a roof over their family's head. The employers did not—could not—see the employees as people; they were numbers, statistics, and profit margins and therefore things to be manipulated and managed, often by gifted bribes disguised as benevolent donations from caring employers. Such noble acts of false generosity were designed to retain the workers' gratitude and loyalty; instead, in their relentless pursuit for greater wealth, these jute barons inadvertently created memorials to their eternal glorification, which merely demonstrated a narcissistic conceit of self-importance.

The Good Old Days

The overall environment and conditions of the workforce were bad, and in some mills deplorably bad; coupled with this were the noise and fine dust of jute fibres that hung in the air like a mist clinging to clothes, skin, and lungs alike. Such conditions also caused acute and even chronic respiratory ailments in later life. In the early twentieth century, the average life expectancy in the working jute community of Dundee was only thirty-two years. It was poignantly pointed out, however, by the jute officials (without embarrassment or humility), that these figures also included child mortality and female deaths due to childbirth. Perhaps this helped alleviate the conscience of the mill masters regarding the threats and dangers endured by each worker each day, for a wage that barely sustained their family's existence. My great-aunt had her eye knocked out by a broken overhead belt, my grandfather was almost completely deaf due to a lifetime of work alongside the noise of machinery in the mills, and a neighbour of mine died prematurely of what was referred to as consumption, again after years of work in the dust of the mills. In these far-off days, no compensation was ever given or offered to any worker who had been injured in the jute industry. If there was any form of remuneration, then it would have been so slight as to be unworthy of mention.

The few workers who decided to strike on occasions due to bad conditions or low wages were dealt with by means of a lockout, which meant that the whole family suffered extreme hardship until the strike was broken. Strike breakers were often engaged to force an end to any dispute. By mutual consent among the mill masters, the ringleaders were then identified and blacklisted, forthwith rendering them unemployable throughout the city. In the meantime, let us not forget that World War I had to be fought, and won, by these same and similar workers in the country. Some called this period of our history "the good old days"? Let's think again!

In the early days (the middle and late nineteenth century), it was not unusual for a child to be chained to their loom to prevent them from leaving their station, and beatings of such children were not an uncommon event during the long, twelve-hour day. Under such notorious conditions, a child would often fall asleep (still in chains), only to be woken with a bucket of cold water thrown over them, a sharp reminder as to their purpose in life.

This was not only a Dundee problem as ill treatment and child labour appeared nationwide. The Lancashire cotton mills were another example where conditions were equally as bad. Circumstances were in many ways even worse for the many children working down the coal mines and on the land. And of course, there were the child chimney sweeps who often died while stuck in the restricted area of a creosote-choked chimney flue. Child chimney sweeps only disappeared as late as 1875 in Britain—and later in the United States. Many of these child labourers were scarred and deformed as a result of the hard work, frequent accidents, and lack of nourishment; many were severely punished and whipped and subjected to all forms of abuse, which frequently resulted in appalling deaths. There was little comeback upon the employer for inflicting such harshness upon children who, if injured or killed, were easily disposed of. Young orphans were often targeted, selected, and fetched from a poorhouse or orphanage (frequently run by the church); they may have been bought or more than likely just given away to their new boss (or owner). This would mean one less mouth for the institution to feed.

Such behaviour was nothing more than indentured labour (slavery), which supposedly had been abolished under the Slavery Abolition Act, 1833 (with the notable exception of the East India Company's controlled territories). Recently there have been suggestions that Britain should apologise for their part in the slave trade. As far as Dundee is concerned, that may apply to the aristocratic families of yesteryear—fine—but not to the working-class and the slave-induced orphans; one enslaved society need not apologize to another.

Despite these conditions, and in what was still dominantly a linen trade, the burgh's population continued to grow, in line with the growth of steam power. It was not until the middle of the nineteenth century that jute became dominant (along with whaling and some shipbuilding). Also, the appearance of the railway network attracted other industries, but regardless of the burgh's overall industrial growth, it was not reflected in the mill worker's wage packet. In 1824, a spinner could earn 10/- per week (50p) for a fifteen-hour day. Nonetheless, by 1850, they were earning only 6/- (30p) per week. This admittedly was for a ten-hour day, but despite the reduction in hours, it still represented a 40 per cent shortfall in earnings. However, due to new technology, these spinners were now expected to attend 120 spindles per frame as opposed to forty in 1824, a threefold increase in production. The workers were being blatantly exploited and underpaid; the mill owners were extracting as much as they could get for as little as they could give. It was little wonder that the Dundee textile workers were tired and discontented.

Despite the overall increase in production, there was an ever-increasing threat from the rival jute centre in East Bengal. Almost immediately, certainly as early as 1855, machinery and men started to be exported from Dundee to Bangladesh, originally by George Achand. There, this coarse fibre could be manufactured cheaper, so Bangladesh quickly became a real threat and rival to the city. Even during the American Civil War and Britain's Boer War, East Bengal received more British contracts for sandbags and ship sails, in preference to Dundee. Nonetheless, it took one hundred years for the final remnants of the Dundee textile industry to fade from the city and disappear. Almost all the machinery and technology that connected this great jute city to its recent past were either scrapped or shipped abroad. One by one, the jute barons left the city to its fate, investing their Dundee-attained profits in far-off Eastern mills. And for the next few decades, many of their great mansions were left abandoned and open to the eroding elements of the Scottish weather. However, their names linger on as Caird Hall, Baxter's Park, and Cox's Stack, all iconic memories to the glorification of their family names but now rightfully belonging to the reminiscences of a withering past. Such brutal memories are fading from the minds of the people on whose backs these jute barons accumulated their bewildering wealth and status.

The Tay Bridge Disaster

John McElroy, my great grandfather from Ireland, had only been in Dundee for a few years when an event occurred that shook the world of engineering and which I, as author of this book, could not ignore. It also acted as a catalyst to a story, told to me by my grandfather, to which John may, or may not, have been connected.

The Tay Bridge Disaster of 1879 is now simply part of Dundee's colourful history, but at the time, it was a nightmare that was impossible to forget. It was one of the great engineering disasters of the nineteenth century and occurred on the last Sunday of the year,

29 December, at exactly 7.16 p.m. The still hands of the watch worn by the locomotive's guard verified the time of the disaster, to the minute. For him, time had stopped as he sank to his death in the dark waters of the River Tay.

Dundee, which at that time was the richest city in Europe, required the rail bridge to link it directly to its southern markets. The bridge was completed in 1878, after which the designer, Thomas Bouch, received a knighthood for his work. But the collapse of the bridge had taken its toll on this devastated man, and he died, at the age of 59, only months after the end of a damming inquiry. The word *botch* (a bungled piece of work) has since then been associated with his name.

The court of inquiry, due to two of its three members being engineers, and so tended to sympathise with the designer, failed to unanimously condemn Bouch. Nevertheless, they concluded that the design, construction, and maintenance all contributed to its collapse. The general opinion of the inquiry was that the foundations and supporting girders, although adequate, depended on the report of a geological survey that wrongly located the river's underlying bedrock. Hence, improvisation to the design was necessary during its construction so the concrete piers that supported the suspended girders of the bridge had to be spaced out more than planned. In addition, there was insufficient supervision during and after completion. Also, defects in the iron castings during the construction were camouflaged by a mixture of cement along with iron filings, referred to as Beaumont egg. This was never reported until the inquiry. During the bridge inspections, cracks and loose diagonal tie bars were frequently observed, causing the bridge to vibrate and shake, which was mostly corrected by iron loops and wedging. To allow for heat expansion (and contraction) of this enormous structure, eleven of the thirteen supporting girders of the central high span were attached to their piers by roller systems. This was potentially catastrophic as severe lateral wind pressure blowing down the Tay Valley had not been allowed for. The first Tay Bridge had been the longest human construction over tidal water (two and a half miles in length), yet despite research compiled in France on large-scale bridge structures, no consideration had been given to the factor of wind pressure. This was also to be the case for the construction of the rail bridge over the River Forth, as Bouch also held the design plans for it. Finally, due to the movement of traffic across the bridge, vibrations were recorded throughout the entirety of the structure. Hence, a compulsory speed limit of twenty-five miles per hour, set by the board of trade, was imposed on all traffic, which was rarely observed and only added to the accumulation of weaknesses. This was a bridge that was doomed from the start, and as these anomalies culminated on that fateful night, the bridge finally fatigued and broke.

Many stories sprang from the disaster, and my grandfather, Steve, often told me a strange tale, which had been passed down from his father, John, about an unknown passenger. There was a disputed total of seventy-five people who perished that night in the freezing waters of the River Tay. Nevertheless, the death toll may only have been fifty-nine, but only forty-six death certificates were issued. This meant that between thirteen and twenty-nine passengers either lay unidentified in the makeshift morgue at the Dundee rail station or were missing in the cold waters of the North Sea. There were no survivors, other than the locomotive itself, which was recovered from the bottom of the river. After a refit, it was renamed the *Diver* and ran for the next forty years.

One of the bodies that was never found was that of an Irishman called Patrick (or just "Paddy" for short). Although my great-grandfather (John) claimed that he never knew Paddy, he frequently recalled that this was not the type of man you would willingly cross. Paddy had escaped police custody in Edinburgh and was on the run. My grandfather claimed that this man was not an Irish nationalist but, like my grandfather, had been a product of the Irish Potato Famine of the mid nineteenth century, during which time Paddy had watched his mother die a slow and lingering death primarily due to the conditions of the time. He never forgot nor forgave the British government for its inaction during those days of extreme hardship. However, attempting to restart his life, he moved to the mainland, settling in Edinburgh. He was unlucky, and things did not go well for this despondent young man, so he deteriorated into a life of petty crime. Burglary, physical assault, and perhaps even murder were levelled against him.

According to John, these were all false allegations raised against his friend and were the product of a secret service, which existed within the police force, whose prime objective was to eke out undesirables; Paddy was one such person. As an uninvited single Catholic man of the right age, from Ireland, whose name happened to be Patrick, what else could he be other than a prime injurious candidate, who perfectly fitted the template pattern of undesirables? He had to be a potential threat against society and therefore a person of interest to these unknown authorities. Paddy had been held for several days in the local tollbooth prison and had expectations of a lengthy sentence of penal servitude followed by extradition back to Ireland. These were not good prospects, so somehow, he had to escape.

His chance of freedom came one day while being transferred between prison blocks. His unsympathetic keepers were threatening to chain him to the wall of the prison by means of the jougs.[1] This was not for Paddy, who although weakened was still strong enough to resist being placed in irons. In the melee that followed, one of the jailers held Paddy in a stranglehold, but he did not have the strength of this determined and furious Irishman. The jailer's hand slipped over the struggling prisoner's face, and it was then that Paddy took his chance; he bit and crunched hard into a restraining finger. The bone cracked and eventually snapped, blood spurted out in all directions, the jailor reared back, more in astonishment than pain. "Oh God! He's bit mi finger aff!" was the cry. Momentarily the tussle stopped, and Paddy was off like a greased bullet.

He quickly lost his pursuers among the narrow alleyways and closes of Edinburgh's old town. At this point, he had no money and no status and depended entirely on his wits, of which he had plenty. Fortunately for renegade Paddy, there was a large Irish settlement in

---

[1]   An iron collar attached by a chain to the outside wall of a prison.

Edinburgh, especially in and around the city's Cowgate area, which had been nicknamed Little Ireland. It was not long before the news of Paddy's daring escape leaked out. This was late summer, and although he had friends who were prepared to help, that help was limited. To a large extent, he lived on petty crime, and after three months living as a criminal, he had had enough. Paddy had spent long enough hiding from the law, and as the cold, damp Edinburgh winter started to set in, he decided that it was time for him to change his ways. It was time for Paddy to move on, to a place where friends could set him up in a job and give him shelter. That place was to be Dundee.

He had arranged to be met, on the platform of the Dundee Tay Bridge Station, by two fellow Irishmen, one of whom may have been my great-grandfather (John). This meeting of course never took place. On the last Sunday evening of that year, 1879, a great storm descended over east Scotland. It was especially bad in the Tay Valley, with strong winds blowing down from the west. Such weather conditions may have helped Paddy elude payment of a rail ticket, as he stealthily avoided the two front carriages, one first and the other second class, for fear that his rough appearance may arouse suspicion. He then boarded the last compartment of four third-class carriages that were attached to the northbound train from Waverley Station. As he patiently sat, it seemed ages before large volumes of steam gushed from the locomotive's pistons. The train slowly moved forward out of the station; Paddy rested against the grimy carriage window and gazed out at the passing lights of the city that had been his home, and prison, for almost a full year. Only then did he feel relaxed and free. Falling back into his seat, he looked forward to his clandestine meeting, and a new future. Little did he know that this was the train fated never to reach its destination.

At around 9.15 p.m., the train slowed and stopped at the Wormit signal box at the southern end of the Tay Bridge. There, the baton that allowed the train to pass over this single-track bridge was passed to the driver. On this extremely stormy and windy night, as the train move slowly out over the two-and-a-half-mile span of open water, picking up speed as it went, no one aboard was remotely thinking of wind factor allowances. In fact, they were excitedly peering through the carriage windows at the approaching lights of Dundee. One young man had bought a ticket simply to cross the bridge with his girlfriend and be that bit longer with her. The couple was probably used to the change in vibration as the train approached the central girders, but this time, the change in vibration was due to something completely different.

An eyewitness who was watching from the signal box explained to the later board of inquiry that he saw the train move out over the bridge. There were sparks from the wheels as they were gripped by the bevelled rail lines that were designed to prevent a carriage from derailing. There was then a flash of light followed by darkness. Also, at that point, telephone communication was lost with Dundee. The Wormit attendant, James Roberts, decided to brave the stormy elements of the night to investigate. As he warily walked and crawled out over the bridge, he held in his heart a most dreaded suspicion and fear. With great caution, he approached the high girder span over the river and was the first to discover, in disbelieving horror, that the bridge was down, and so was an entire train.

Being in the end compartment, Paddy may have been the last person to realise what was happening, but on that stormy night, his fate was the same as his fellow passengers as they hit the hostile waters of the ice-cold Tay. His body was never identified. He may have been one of the unclaimed bodies that lay in the makeshift mortuary in the waiting room at Tay Bridge Station. But as nobody appeared to match his description, the chances were that he had been one of the twenty-seven lost forever, washed out into their watery graves in the North Sea.

I was told this story many times by my grandfather, who in turn had heard it from his father. Whether John was one of the two men who were to meet Paddy at the station, he never confirmed or denied. However, he always claimed that the story was true, and my grandfather certainly believed it. And so do I.

The Tay Bridge disaster has been greatly publicised over the last one hundred years, with comparatively little said about its replacement. This new bridge had risen from the rubble of the old in less than eight years, and in its time, it was the true marvel of the engineering world. Designed by William Henry Barlow and built by William Arrol (builder of the famous Forth Bridge), the new Tay Bridge was opened in 1887. It has now stood for approximately 150 years and still has many more years of active service. This bridge stands where the old one fell, with only the stumps of the original foundations appearing above the water level. They are stark reminders of man's frailty and nature's infallibility.

The Old Tay Rail Bridge stumps.

CHAPTER 5

Early Times

A Chance Meeting

It was with tears in his eyes that John McElroy, my maternal great-grandfather, stood along with his sister, Maggie, at the stern of a small ferryboat as it buffeted its way across the choppy Irish Sea. As they left the Port of Larne, in the county of Antrim, they gazed back, for the last time, at Ireland, the land of their birth, and undoubtedly wondered how things had come about. How had such a tragic and calamitous situation been allowed to unfold? The agricultural base of the Irish economy, between 1845 and 1849, had been allowed to virtually collapse. This was due to successive years of crop failure caused by a potato blight, which left the country with nothing to offer but starvation and needless poverty for its people. This was the Irish Potato Famine.

The central government in London, by intent, gave little to no help for the famine victims. By policy, an entire country had been abandoned and left to simply starve. But this was the nineteenth century, when life was still cheap. It was a time when land and profits were ranked above people, at least by the mostly Protestant landlords over the Catholic crofters. It would therefore be fair to say that almost all the Irish immigrants who settled abroad were Catholic. They had left their country due to the harsh treatment inflicted upon them by uncaring absentee landowners, who were represented by their famously corrupt "middlemen." They in turn could extract as much as possible from the already impoverished tenant farmers, who had only enough money left for a single potato harvest. When the blight finally struck, the impact was catastrophic; there was no ensuing war, plague, or geological disaster—only greed—and this resulted in around 1.5 million dead crofters due to starvation. It is strange that this episode in British imperial history has been so glibly passed over.

To escape the severity and ties of the old country, and like so many of the country's youth, John decided to emigrate to greener pastures. However, the new and better life that he sought only took him across the Irish Sea to Scotland, in fact, to the city of Dundee, where he had friends and was offered a job as an Irish navy working on the city's newest bypass, the Hawkhill. While on this short journey from Larne to Stranraer, he met and befriended a priest called Father Stephen Keenan, a name that was to be so important to his future family. John settled on the outskirts of Dundee in a small village called Lochee, named after a loch, just to its north-east side. The next step in his quest for a better way of life was to find a more secure job, which he did, starting work in one of the city's many jute mills.

John had always been musically inclined and had learnt the rudiments of playing the cornet. With a little practice and probably to further secure his job, he joined the work's brass band, something that was later to cost him. Like most men of his age, he met and courted a few young local lasses. But one, by the name of Mary Ann Mudie McDonald, who was also a jute worker in the same mill as John, took his eye. Mary was destined to become his wife, and before long, they had a son, my grandfather, who was named Steven Keenan McElroy. He was born in 1880 and named after the Irish priest his father had befriended.

By this time, John (my great-grandfather) had become an accomplished cornet player and had joined the new local trades' brass band, who were invited to play at Queen Victoria's Golden Jubilee celebrations in Edinburgh (1887). He, along with the rest of the band, stood for over five hours in the cold and pouring rain while waiting for Victoria to arrive. Two days later, he contracted pneumonia, and within a few weeks, he had died.

The course of history had played out badly for this man forced to leave his poverty-stricken homeland, only to work in the nineteenth-century jute mills of Dundee; even Victoria's jubilee was a dark omen for John. Of course, there was no compensation or assurances for his wife. So, like many other mothers and grandmothers, Mary Ann had to fend for herself. After Steve's unexpected death, this young widow, from then on, was remembered as the well-dressed elderly lady who was always seen in mourning black.

When John died, Ireland was still in effect well and truly part of the British Empire; he never saw his homeland take its independence. In fact, it was not until the 1919–21 Irish War of Independence that a bill was passed (in 1920), the Government Act of Ireland, which instigated the creation of two states, both still part of the United Kingdom. The intent was that the two Irelands would reunify later, but of course, this never occurred. By 1922 the Anglo-Irish Treaty created Southern Ireland (Eire) as a self-governing state. It was not surprising that Southern Ireland became a republic in 1949, leaving behind the British and the British Commonwealth. It became a member of the European Community in 1973. Northern Ireland, of course, has remained part of the United Kingdom.

The Young McElroy Family

Although Catholic Ireland was still part of Great Britain, the Irish rightly felt that they were no longer beholden in any way to the Westminster government. The Great Famine was still fresh in many an Irish mind, along with their abandonment and the deceit of British administration. So particularly in the north of the island, where many Protestant families had settled, relations between Catholic and Protestant factions were often at tinderbox tension, ready to explode at a moment's notice. This hostility often transferred itself to the mainland of Britain and continued for decades. In Dundee, Catholics often found it difficult to progress beyond the status of a millworker or that of a road navy. Firms, including D C Thomson, openly refused to employ Catholics, and it was against this difficult background that John's son, my grandfather Steven, met his future wife, Mary McDonald. She, like Steve, was a millworker; however, their respective families came from opposite ends of the religious spectrum. Mary's family included staunch Scottish Protestants, whereas Steve's relatives were equally devout Irish Catholics, a potentially harmful situation for any couple. But Mary, like so many Dundee women of that era, was strong, independent, and free-spirited. There was plenty of employment for the young, nimble-fingered Dundee females in the jute mills, and such women were often the only breadwinners in the family, leading to many strong-minded autonomous women well ahead of their time. My grandmother was one such woman, and she had decided that Steve McElroy was to be her husband, and that was that. Nothing and no one would stop her. She even converted to Catholicism in the process, a courageous step for any woman in those days.

Such a religious switch was frowned upon from both families; a mixed marriage was normally not an option and often spelt trouble. As a young boy, I remember being told how the ideological battle lines were drawn between the two families, accompanied by aggressive posturing between the males. Steve was on his own, but he stood his ground and stuck to his girl. The couple were in love, and family feuding was not going to destroy what they had. He placed no pressure upon his future wife as she prepared to convert to the Catholic faith. Strangely, this apparent willingness by Mary to embrace change was enough to reduce the resentment among her family members, and with good sense prevailing, they felt obliged to respect their daughter's decision. However, I often suspect that such a reciprocal gesture would not have been so forthcoming from Steve. We'll never know.

Except on special occasions, both families always kept a respectful distance of disassociation, but this marriage, which was held in January 1900, was an exception. The groom's and bride's guests attended this very Catholic wedding, after which, during the wedding breakfast, both Catholic and Protestants sat in each other's company and spoke as if they were old close friends.

The young married couple had rented a house in Paterson Street, on the slopes of the Dundee Law. At one time, its steep slopes were on the outskirts of the city, but by the time my mother arrived, they were well within its boundaries. She was born on 24 October 1903 and was christened Betsy McDonald McElroy; however, to prevent confusion with her aunt, whom she had been named after, she was referred to as Bessie, and this name stayed with her for the rest of her life. There was an older sister, Maria, so Bessie was the second sibling born into the family. They were the only grandchildren so were readily spoiled, particularly so by their maternal grandmother and their aunt Maggie, their father's sister. They would often dress the sisters in identical clothes and, being so alike, were often mistaken as twins.

One Easter Sunday, the girls were dressed in their best outfits, which included bonnets and black-laced boots. Their father, Steve, as a treat after chapel, decided to take them to the top of the Dundee Law. This was a favourite Easter venue for Dundee families. Each family had their own picnic, and on the evening prior to this event, they had placed hard-boiled fresh farm eggs into a teapot while the tea was brewing. This stained the eggs brown, after which they would roll each egg down the side of the steep slopes of the Law, a tradition that symbolised the rolling of the stone from Christ's tomb. I remember my grandfather telling me that often the crowds were so thick on the Law that one could not see the grass for the people, and that was the case on this Easter Sunday.

At this time of year, the weather, especially in Scotland, has always been unpredictable, and this year was no exception. The weather could not have staged itself any better. After only minutes on the hilltop, the "heavens opened" and down poured the rain and snowy hail. Until then, it had been a blue, sunny sky; the downpour was so sudden that everyone had been caught off guard. Women were screaming, men were shouting, and children were crying as they were uplifted by their parents and carried down the now slippery slopes of the hill. As the mass exodus got under way, picnics were left abandoned for the birds to pick over at their leisure. With no sheltered haven from the elements on the summit, my grandfather, like the rest of the fathers, picked up his siblings and, with one in each arm, dashed down the entire length of the hill, which at that time was part of the treeless countryside. Fortunately, he was a fit man and ran from the flat summit without stopping until he and his daughters safely reached home, in Patterson Street. By this time, they were soaked from head to toe; bonnets had become sodden strands of straw, and dresses were drenched through to the skin. But it was great fun and something to remember, although their mother thought differently. She was standing at the door, towels in hand and glowering at my father. "Yah daft ald man,"[2] she said, "takin them up the La we nah coats. Yir'a drookit."[3]

Most Sundays, after chapel, the two sisters, one on either side of their father, would set off on a long walk through the city centre and its parks. Steve was a popular man. Although unassuming, he was highly thought of; even strangers as they passed by would nod and tip their hats, which every man wore, and bid him "Good day." A conversation would often ensue. The girls felt that such encounters lasted for ages, as both parties chatted away as if they had known each other for years. However, during such pauses to the Sunday mooch, there were advantages; admiring passers-by often thought they were twins and would sometimes slip them a halfpenny each.

Each Sunday, Steve would routinely sit on the same public bench in the park and watch the sisters play on the grass. However, these Sunday walks would always finish in the same way with two sleepy girls being carried all the way home by their father. To them, this was the norm—long days that always seemed to be summer when the sun shone, and it was constantly warm. They had great love for their father; they thought he was the kindest and wisest man in all the

---

[2]   "You daft old man."

[3]   "Taking them up the Law without coats. You're absolutely soaked."

world. Each day was secure and safe. My mother thought that those far-off days would last forever.

Little did she know what the future held.

The Last Memory of Maria

These long-past recollections of family history seemed to consist of mostly pleasant memories. But not all were pleasant. Tragedy and personal loss were accepted as common occurrences, as my mother often recalled the last sad memory she had of her sister. Maria was sitting up in her small bed, crying and holding her arms out to her mother. Only days later, she died of diphtheria, which then was almost always fatal. She was only 6 years old. Part of Bessie's life had gone; her older sister, who stood beside her when she was frightened and when being scolded by their mother, was no longer there. Bessie had copied everything that her older sister did and followed her everywhere; she was now alone.

Death and tragedy seemed to be more acceptable in those days. Friends and family were closer and more supportive, especially during times of bereavement. The whole family had been affected by Maria's death. It was their first loss. Nevertheless, they had to recover, and quickly. For survival, getting back to work was of the utmost importance, and normal living had to be resumed as soon as possible. The mill masters only allowed one day off work for a funeral of a close relative—without pay. If one took longer, then it could cost one's job, which was easily filled. This was a modified industrial feudal system whereby the mill masters had little interest in, or sympathy for, the well-being of their employees beyond their productive potential. The bereaved were simply expected to adjust, so little love was lost between employer and employee. It was as if the workers had no feelings; in fact, the working class displayed more genuine love within their family circles than any of the mill masters, who were often more concerned about asset distribution at the time of any bereavement.

Bessie was simply too young to understand the finality of death and probably adjusted more easily and coped better with the death of Maria than did her parents. But even in her old age, Bessie clearly remembered that part of her shared childhood: her sister's face, her voice, and her whole memory so sad and so vivid. As a young girl, she remembered and lamented but never quite understood the passing of her sister and best friend. Each time I was told that story, she would remark, "I wonder what life would have been like if Maria had survived." And then with a slight smile and a teardrop in the corner of her eye, she would say, "If I had grown up with an older sister, maybe we would have grown old together." Maybe?

CHAPTER 6

The Walkie

A New Start

Not long after Maria's passing, the family moved to a tenement flat on the slopes of Dallfield Walk ("the Walkie). It was a slightly larger house and much closer to the city's centre and Steve's work. This was the house in which Bessie's parents spent the rest of their lives together. It was known as a "but-n-ben," which consisted of only two rooms; the backroom was used as the bedroom for Bessie. In addition to this, it was also the room that was kept for only special occasions so was rarely used. The front room was the living room area where all the action took place. It was the living space, usually around the kitchen table, where they also ate. The mother and father also slept here, in the double bed, which fitted into the alcove in the corner. The house was one level up in a three-storey tenement, with an outside communal toilet (or watery, as the older generation called it). This was shared with three neighbouring families on the same level (or platy). For the watery, all four families had a key, which was usually hung on a hook inside their front door. In those days, toilet paper was an expensive luxury. Instead, newspapers were used, cut into rectangular sheets, and sewn through by a piece of jute yarn, which was then hung onto a nail hammered into the rough-brick toilet wall. There was not a tap water basin, and of course, there was no hot water supply. In fact, for the whole tenement, the only form of heating or lighting was through gas pipes.

To light up a darkened room, one required a long-tapered candle. Once set alight, it would be held up to a small muslin bag (or mantle) attached to a gas bracket set over the fireplace. The gas supply was then turned on and the mantle would fill with gas, which would then immediately ignite. A pure-white glow then filled the room, and with a quiet hiss from the mantle, a soft air of tranquillity would spread to every corner, something that modern electric lights don't achieve. When igniting the mantle, timing was of the essence; applying the burning taper too soon would cause the expensive fragile mantle to burn out, but any delay would cause unburnt gas to escape, which once ignited could cause a gas-flash singeing one's hair and eyebrows. On very few and rare occasions, an explosion could occur, and in more extreme and exceptional circumstances, a house could be blown to pieces, even bringing down the entire tenement.

Of course, this did not only apply to gas lighting; the gas cooker was also a source of extreme danger, as my grandmother once found out. She, having been distracted, forgot (for the first time, and almost the last) that the gas supply to the cooker had been turned on but not lit. On her return, she lit the taper and placed it into the cooker, whereupon it ignited, but not in the way she had expected. With a tremendous exploding bang that rendered my grandmother temporarily deaf, the top rings of the cooker were blown upwards into the roof, where they were embedded; the two cast iron side panels of the cooker blew outwards, one into the coal bunker below the window and the other into the wall of the backroom. On the other side of this wall, which was Bessie's bedroom, my grandfather was quietly sitting while looking out of the window. The cast iron door ripped forward like a cannonball into the room recess, where my grandparents' bed resided (in the same room as the cooker). My grandmother, who was standing just to one side of the cooker door, missed the entire impact of the explosion. If she had been standing only a few inches in front of the door, she would have received the full impact. Shocked and deafened, she stood completely still until her hearing gradually came back. Her first thoughts were for Steve as one whole side of the cooker had ripped into the bedroom wall where he was sitting. Rushing in to see what had happened to her husband, she was met with a smile. "Oh, hello, wife," he said turning around. "Did yi hear that tyre burst." Then to add insult to injury, he asked if the dinner was ready. The response was quick. "Yi daft auld man, a wis nearly blan oot o the windee."[4] As he entered the living room and saw the bedraggled state of Mary, his response was unassumingly bland. "Mi god wuman this is an afy cerry on yr hayn. Ar' yi a richt?"[5] The conversation after that was not for our ears, but I can tell you that it was very one-sided and loud. However, by night-time, they were sitting together by the coal fire having a wee natter (or crack) with each other.

Of course, family and friends had to be told every detail of the escapade, and as time slowly separated the event from the true story, it grew steadily more ridiculous and amusing. Nonetheless, Mary was lucky to have survived. They both managed to live into their eighties, during which they continued with their nightly cracks.

The Bond Fire

As the months passed, Maria's death had become a faded memory to young Bessie, who was spending more time with her father. In fact, the first memory after the loss of her sister was of him. It was one evening (19 July 1906) when Steve lifted Bessie onto his shoulders and pointed to a large red and blue glow in the sky. "Look," he said. "That's the Bond fire. Don't forget that you've seen it." Of course, she had no idea what the Bond was but never forgot his words or what she saw. She recalled blue waves of flame shooting into the sky, fringed with red and yellow, all of which appeared to be sitting

---

[4]   "You daft old man, I was nearly blown out of the window."
[5]   "My god, woman, this is a terrible carryon you're having. Are you all right?"

on a steady, deep-red glow. Bessie remembered no sound, just the glowing fireball over the centre of the city. The Bond was James Watson's bonded warehouse, where many whisky vats were stored. The heat was so intense that the vats, filled with the pure, golden liquid (whisky), exploded, causing a great local catastrophe. Dundee was a city filled with highly inflammable jute products, so sudden and intense fires were nothing new, but this was by far the largest in its history, perhaps with the notable exception of the Hill town district. Here, allegedly in 1689, this first suburb of Dundee was burnt from end to end. The incendiary was the viscount of Dundee, John Graham of Claverhouse (better known as Bonnie Dundee). This was punishment in response to the inhabitant's refusal to open the city gates on the arrival of his Jacobite army.

By the next day, the Bond fire had burnt itself out; nevertheless, there was still a strong, sweet smell from the whisky-saturated embers that continued to smoulder, the smoke of which wafted across the city's centre. Bessie and her father walked the half mile down from their house on Dallfield Walk to the Seagate, where the warehouse once stood. Amidst the smoke, glass bottles could be seen littering the road. Due to the intensity of the fire, they had been distorted into strange, agonising shapes, now frozen in time. These useless remnants were the only reminder of a night filled with fire and fear. Some people took these twisted misshapen bottles as mementoes, but Steve, being the honest upright man that he was, would touch nothing. His honesty always stood out in Bessie's mind, and I think that it became the standard by which she judged others, often unfairly. He was certainly an intelligent man, an ardent reader and fast at mental arithmetic. His cognitive skills were so good that his fellow workers in the mill would trust him to check their wage packet at the end of each working week. In his head, he would tally up their hours, along with any overtime, and immediately tell if there was a mistake.

A Day to Remember

Another memorable day to remember while on the Dallfield Walk occurred when Bessie was only 8 years old. The family had settled into their new home, and on this precise day, Bessie was off school. She recollected that her father, during a period of idleness, came rushing into the house completely out of breath. With great excitement, he announced that Jack Johnson was here in Dundee. His wife, Mary, had no idea who Jack Johnson was so was not impressed by this revelation. However, Steve, in his euphoria, grabbed his jacket and dashed out of the house; Mary was astonished and had to sit down as she had never seen Steve in such a state. After composing herself, she ran to the back-room window, from where she saw Steve disappear up the Walkie and along McDonald Street. A neighbour had seen Steve run up the Walkie and Mary looking out of her window. "Ah, Jack Johnson in toon?" the neighbour shouted up. "Wha's Jack Johnson?" asked Mary. "Oh, he's some boxer that won something." This seemed to satisfy Mary, and the two women then started to gossip about something else.

Jack Johnson was in town, but he was not just any boxer. It was 1911, and this visitor to the city happened to be the heavyweight boxing champion of the world, and the first black man ever to hold that title. Due to the intense racial animosity that existed in his homeland of America and an alleged misdemeanour, he fled his homeland along with his white wife, Lucille. His decision to come to Dundee was a spontaneous choice and came after a conversation with a fellow traveller (Sydney McLaglen) during a flight to Newcastle, where Johnson was due to box. He had long wanted to become a member of the Order of Free Masonry, but prejudice feelings in America against the black man had put a stop to that. However, he joined the Forfar and Kincardine Lodge No. 225, Dundee, on 13 October 1911. The Grand Lodge of Scotland, under instructions from the Grand Lodge of America, was ordered to suspend and stop the proceedings. However, Lodge 225 had deliberately locked the doors before the start of the ceremony and received no such communication. As a result, the lodge was subsequently suspended, but the deed had been done and John Arthur "Jack" Johnson was carried out shoulder high by his fellow Masons. Word had spread that the heavyweight boxing champion was present in the city, and a large crowd had gathered outside the lodge, my grandfather being one. He, along with the rest of the cheering and applauding assemblage of Dundonians, marched the champion all the way to the rail station. Johnson was reported to have said that this was the most glorious time of his life.

Four-Legged Friends

Although young, Bessie soon became an outgoing child who loved accompanying her mother almost everywhere. She particularly enjoyed washday, which involved climbing from Dallfield Walk up part of the Dundee Law, which at that time was part of the countryside. Its lower part was crisscrossed by fields of different shapes and sizes, all only a few acres in size and in which cattle often grazed. They were mainly there to keep the grass down and at the same time fertilise the ground. In one field, part of which is still there, stood a communal brick-built washhouse, not far from Patterson Street, where the family had once lived. For a while, Bessie's mother, Mary, continued to do the family's weekly wash in this washhouse. It was a long walk from Dallfield Walk, but her old neighbours were there, and it was difficult for her to lose contact. Also, she enjoyed the chat.

Here, the working mothers and wives congregated on Friday evening to do their family wash and keep up with the latest news and, of course, scandal. Bessie was always placed into the field, next to the washhouse, where she played happily in the grass while the women did their weekly wash and gossiped. To complete this tranquil setting, there were a few grazing cows in the far corner of the field. However, the peace was about to be shattered. While Bessie played, one of these docile animals decided to stroll over and investigate this new arrival. At first, Bessie did not notice this lumbering, inquisitive beast as she sat in the warm sunshine content and amusing herself with a small Eskimo doll that she called *dukka* (Icelandic for "doll"). It was a present from her uncle Albert, who was a whaler and part of the large Dundee whaling fleet. It was when the cow licked her with its large, rough, slobbering tongue that the trouble started. Convinced that the cow had bitten her on the head, she screamed. Her mother immediately recognised her daughter's voice; it was loud enough, and she had heard it often. Mary immediately dropped her washing and along with the rest of the women ran out.

Thinking something terrible had happened, they were met with a passive, unassuming cow licking Bessie. Mary, along with the rest of the women, immediately burst into laughter, probably with relief. "The coos only tryen ti be friendly,"[6] she said through her laughter. But Bessie would not have it. "Look am bleedin" she insisted. "Yir no bleedin at'a. It's only the dumb breat's slavers. It's drooled a oor yi. Noo come awa inside yi daft gouk"[7] was the mother's reply. Although the cow did not bite her, one thing was certain, blood or no blood, cow, or no cow: Bessie never played in that field again. Shortly after this, Mary became tired of walking that distance each Friday and transferred her weekly wash to the much closer washhouse in the meadows at the bottom of Constitution Brae.

Once properly settled in Dallfield Walk, Bessie's life changed forever; James (Jim), a baby brother, was born. She now had a younger brother tagging along behind, so there was someone else to be responsible for, which had far-reaching consequences for her.

She had not long started attending school (around 5 years old) when she, along with Jim, had another encounter with a four-legged beast, but this time it was not a cow. One sunny afternoon, Bessie was happily playing with Jim and a few friends at the top of the Walkie Brae. Nearby, an enormous Clydesdale horse was being harnessed in preparation for its day's work. There was nothing unusual in this; horses were a common site in the city as they drew heavy jute loads

---

6   "The cow is only trying to be friendly."
7   "You're not bleeding at all. It's only the dumb animal's saliva. It's drooled all over you. Now come away inside, you silly girl."

through the Dundee streets. So little notice was taken of either the horse or the carter. But suddenly, Bessie felt herself being lifted high into the air and placed on the horse's back. At first, she didn't realise what was happening or where she was going. To her, she was a mile high. That was fine, but then the horse moved. On realising her predicament, she immediately released one of the loudest yells ever heard on Dallfield Walk. Windows opened, and heads peered out to see what the commotion was about. Had a cart broken loose and was it now careening out of control down the steep Dallfield Brae and about to hurtle into 'Goalys' pub at the bottom of the hill? Or did someone fall from the top storey of one of the numerous tenements?

No! It was a little girl sitting on a horse's back who did not want to be there. The carter quickly lifted her from this lofty position and placed her promptly back on the pavement. With her brother in tow, she immediately took off down the hill and home, no doubt to the great relief of both her and the carter, who sheepishly waved to the onlooking spectators that all was well. The children all knew the carter and his horse, and they were used to being lifted on and off its back—but not Bessie. She did enjoy riding on the back of an empty cart alongside the rest of the kids, but that was where it stopped; sitting so high up on the back of a horse was out of the question. It was after this traumatising drama that she gave, for a long time, all large four-legged animals a wide berth.

Almost the whole of the city was built on the slopes of the Law, and many of the north-south running streets were inclined at an extremely steep angle, Dallfield Walk being no exception. One of the first memories of the Walkie that indelibly stuck in my mother's mind for the rest of her life occurred one cold, autumn day when a hard frost had covered the smooth, cobbled roads with a thin layer of ice. This was fun for the young ones, some of whom created ice slides that often ran the whole length of the Walkie. It was not so much fun for the cart horses who, when laden with enormous heavy bails of jute, were expected to ascend (and more dangerously descend) the streets of a city riddled with extremely steep hills.

The horse on whose back Bessie was placed several months before was of the large Clydesdale breed; he was related to the famous Dundee cart horse called Bullar after General Bullar of the Boer War. Such horses were expected to pull a full cartload of jute no matter what the weather was like. Bessie said that she felt so sorry for those poor beasts of burden, as they always appeared to be so sad. In winter, the roads were often covered in snow and ice, and a horse would struggle downhill. In such conditions, barbed boots would be tethered to the horse's hoofs and heavy chains would be tied round the wheel rims of the carts, helping to prevent them from skidding out of control, but sometimes this was not enough. Also, instead of granite cobbles, wooden blocks were laid on the road at warehouse entrances and dockland areas, designed to prevent a fire caused by sparks from the scarifying shoes of a horse. However, often a horse would temporarily lose its footing when crossing over from one road surface type to another.

Bessie's horse was fully loaded and had just come from the McDonald Street warehouse on its way to one of the mills in the west end of the city. It had manoeuvred out of a wooden-floored warehouse when it slipped on the granite cobbled surface of Dallfield Brae. Bessie remembered seeing the horse stagger as it attempted to hold its footing on the slippery road on its way downhill. The weight of the fully loaded cart was too much, and immediately the cart skidded and the horse went down on its side. The heavy bails of jute tumbled forward on top of the animal, and in desperation, it tried to rise but could not. Again, and again, it tried, but all was in vain. Bessie saw the eyes of the horse bulge out from its head as it looked round towards its master, the carter. He ran forward and held the iron bit in the mouth of the horse, to calm his old friend down.

By this time, many of the young men from the Walkie had organised themselves and were removing the heavy jute bails. This was not an unusual occurrence in the city, and the Dundonians knew exactly how to respond. The poor horse lay quietly on its side until all the bails were unloaded. Although frightened and in pain, it seemed to understand that it was being helped. The next step was to get the horse back onto its feet, else it would simply give up. It was then that disaster struck. My mother said that she heard the carter give out a loud cry. The old horse tried to rise on its own but was too weak. It fell back and appeared to go into spasm. Its hind leg went into contraction and then it kicked out, after which the horse lay still.

There was absolute silence on the Walkie. They knew that the poor beast had gone into shock and there was nothing they could do. The carter hung his arms round the huge neck of his old and only companion; he knew that his friend was dying. The carter rose to his feet, stroked the horse's white main, and then, with great dignity, walked away. Bessie recalled that by this time, word had spread, and an official-looking man had appeared on the scene. He was dressed in a tidy but shabby suit and wore a bowler hat. He also held a long sinister-looking instrument in his hand. He was either a vet or—more than likely—a butcher from the slaughterhouse (abattoir) and the instrument he held was a bolt gun for stunning and killing animals. No time was lost, and only seconds after his appearance, a jute cover was placed over the stricken animal's head. This was followed by a loud, sharp crack through the air and then a deafening silence; the trembling body of the animal then shuddered for the last time. The horse was dead.

The carter was standing beside a few men during these final moments of his companion's life. There was no compensation or insurances, and on that fateful morning, the carter had lost his horse, his friend, and his livelihood. He was no longer a carter, which was not so much a job but more a way of life, giving him a degree of standing within the community. He would now have to find a job in the mills. This was not an infrequent event on the steep braes of Dundee; all able men of the city knew what to do, but they also knew what to expect. If the horse got back on its feet, which was on most occasions, things would end in a cheer from the crowd, but not this time. The small gathering that was left dispersed in silence. There was no hero that day, just a dead horse and a distraught man who had once been a carter.

A Trip up the River

John McDonald was my mother's maternal grandfather. He was a master butcher, which meant that he and his wife were relatively well off. Their family consisted of three sons and a daughter, and they lived in Castle Court in the centre of the city, an area which was becoming of the of status of a master butcher. This whole area of the city was demolished in the 1930s to make way for Dundee's Caird Hall and City Square. John originally belonged to the village of Stanley, where he was well respected for his butchering skills. Farmers throughout the county sought his services, bringing their cattle to be slaughtered and then butchered by him. He was therefore expected to maintain a certain social standing in the community.

Belonging to the Church of Scotland, he was expected to attend morning and afternoon Sunday services, which he did with somewhat uncharacteristic enthusiasm. Having attended the morning service, he would again prepare himself for the afternoon. So, with his best suit, top hat, gloves, and Bible under his arm, John would stride off. Eventually, his wife, Mary Ann (or just Annie), who knew him all too well, suspected that something was not quite right. His enthusiasm and regularity for an afternoon church service were well out of character. So, she decided that an investigation was required to find out exactly what he was up to.

The next Sunday, Annie, allowed her husband to prepare as usual. Immaculately dressed, he set out of for the kirk, but this time, she followed. She closely shadowed him into the town, but he turned not towards the church. Instead, he walked towards the riverfront. In fact, straight to the boat wharf, where his butcher colleagues were waiting. They planned, as they did each Sunday, to have a boozy sail up the river to the small village of Newburgh on the banks of the Tay. Then, presumably to return home, full of the spirit. It was not to be, at least for this husband on this Sunday or, as Annie intended, any other Sunday from then on. At that point, she pounced and demanded that he come off the boat at once. "Awa hame Annie," said an embarrassed John, "and no mack a fail o' me."[8] But Annie, who was a religious person, was not for going home. "Come aff that boat, John McDonald, or a'll jump in the river" was her immediate response. John knew when he was beat and respectfully gave into his wife's wishes, sheepishly coming off the boat and home. His weekly trip up the river was foiled, at least for the time being.

After the death of John, my mother asked if she would have jumped. Annie shook her head. "No likely. Ah canny sweem and neither kin John, onywey weed beth been drookit, ah jist wanted ti fleg him."[9] Did he ever sail up the river with his cronies again? Who knows?

In years to come, on request from Bessie, Annie would often open the large chest that sat in the corner of her room and show her John's top hat, gloves, and suit—the same ones that were worn on that day by the river. Also in the chest, she kept her wedding dress, still wrapped in its original paper.

Almost a year to the day after this event, the whole family was stunned when John unexpectedly died, particularly due to the shocking nature of his death. The butchers in those days were a closely knit group who frequently met in secret, such as that Sunday afternoon jaunt up the river. On such occasions, the butchers had a reputation of consuming a great deal of alcohol. After one such meeting, John arrived home in a state of absolute inebriation, and his wife decided that the best place for him was bed. On his way up the staircase towards the bedroom, he slipped and fell back down the full flight of stairs. His neck was broken, and he died instantly.

This was a catastrophe for the whole family. They had lost a good father, but it was particularly tragic for Annie. She had not only lost her husband, but had no other form of income, widows' pensions being non-existent. With no prospects or solution in sight, she was

---

8   "Go home, Annie, and don't make a fool of me."
9   "Not likely. I cannot swim, and neither could John. Anyway, we would have been soaked through. I just wanted to give him a fright."

left to bring up her six young children alone. The Parish Council helped those who were in dire need, but Annie's case was not extreme enough. Due to her assets, she was above the poverty level and was therefore subject to means testing by the parish. They insisted that she sell all her nonessential assets and live on the proceeds until nothing was left, after which, the parish would consider her claim. Everything was sold, including the bed, her table, and her chairs, and even the waxcloth that covered the floor was now too fancy for her new impoverished lifestyle. To add mocking insult to her injured pride, many of her previous friends sat in judgement on the Parish Council. Sisters, brothers, uncles, and all sides of the family tried to help, but they had little enough for themselves. Eventually, Annie put together some assemblage of a home. She went back to the jute mills and worked a twelve-hour day, after which she took in and did other family's washing; in this way, she avoided the dreaded East House. This was the poorhouse and was a place where no rightminded person wanted to be. It was where destitute families were placed and inevitably broken up. But Annie somehow managed to keep her family together without a man's wage. She once told my mother, "Ah work ah day an ah work ah night, and noo Bessie, am tired."[10] In time, things took their toll.

Mary Ann (Annie)

Mary Ann lived on for a long time after John's death, but she never forgot her treatment at the hands of her pseudo insincere Protestant friends, who made up part of the Parish Council. She switched allegiance to Catholicism having found more comfort in her Catholic neighbours. Eventually, she took a but-in-ben flat on Dallfield Walk opposite the family home. This was convenient for the whole family, and my mother as a young girl would often spend many nights with her grandmother, which helped reduce the pressure

---

[10]   "I work all day and I work all night and now, Bessie, am tired."

of overcrowding in her parents' home. It was also company for Mary Ann, and Bessie ran most of her gran's errands, which included fetching the daily flagon of milk from the local dairy. This flagon, which every household possessed, held a quart of milk (just under a litre) and was heavy for a 7-year-old, but Bessie would swing the container repeatedly around and over her head until she reached her aunt's home. She delivered the milk without ever spilling a single drop, or so she said. The reward was the odd biscuit and occasional sweet, a great treat then.

Mary Ann's staunch Catholic belief was not lost on either Bessie or her younger brother, Jim. At precisely twelve noon each day, and just as the bells of St Mary's Chapel in Forebank Road rang out, she would call out, summoning almost in a subpoena-type fashion, her two grandchildren. They would wait for the ringing tone of their aunt's voice then would urgently hurry up the tenement stairs and along the landing in a race to finally stand, completely out of breath, in her living room all before the twelfth toll of the bell. Once inside, fun and games stopped, the atmosphere became solemn, and earnest Mary Ann knelt on both knees. The children did likewise as they dutifully said their daily prayers. Such an affectionate act of faith, particularly among Catholics, was commonplace in those days, but alas, not so much now. I feel that such a loss of devotion has significantly wounded society. Nevertheless, having said this, I very much doubt if Mary (Bessie's mother) ever prayed to any great extent. Now a Catholic, she told Bessie, with a twinkle in her eye and a smile on her face, "Ah just wanted ti marry yer father."[11] Well, she did, and the marriage did him no harm—and probably some good.

During the long, winter nights, Mary Ann often felt lonely so Bessie would stay overnight. Both would look forward to this except, for one small detail. Each morning Mary Ann would rise early to attend the five o'clock mass, which meant that Bessie was alone in the house. She was young, and any unusual noise would send this frightened girl trembling beneath the bed covers. The quivering

---

[11] "I just wanted to marry your father."

shadows caused by the flicker of a candle that always sat at the bedside did not help matters as she saw strange figures leaping from wall to wall and imagined them to be shapeless beings dancing to the shimmering light of the candle. Bessie, with great courage, would eventually lift herself up and by the light of a single taper search below the bed, in the wardrobe, and behind the curtains. What she was looking for was not quite clear, and what she would have done if found, I have no idea.

Only after this painstaking search, which included inside of the coal bunker, did Bessie climb back into bed, where she lay apparently hidden below the sheets. She could have set the house on fire, but of course, that was the last thing on her mind at the time. Mary Ann's excursions to early morning chapel were finally made known to the family, and this marked the end of my mother's overnight stays. Her gran was never told the reason why these visits were stopped. Instead, elaborate excuses were made to prevent these night ventures from ever occurring again.

Annie's Death

It happened during a fine sunny Saturday, and as the women would say, "There was a fine drying wind." Annie decided to hang out her washing, which involved climbing onto of the coal bunker, which was always situated at the window. The washing itself was hung outside in the open air by means of a rope-and-pully system. This was attached to a tall, communal, wooden pole (the greenie pole), which often stood as high as four storeys and was situated in the back green, serving all the families in that tenement.

On this day, Annie, after climbing on top of the bunker with her washing basket, accidentally staggered and stepped onto the washing board at her feet and slipped. She fell backwards onto the hard floor, dislocating her hip, from which she never recovered. Annie by then was an elderly woman and as a result was confined to her bed, in agony, for six long weeks before finally succumbing to her injury. It was not until her sisters and Mary, her daughter-in-law, were dressing and preparing her for the funeral that the dislocation and truth were discovered. The doctor attending Annie failed either to inform the family of her injured hip or take any measures to help her. Instead, this brave woman who had worked so hard to keep her family together lay in agony for six weeks, until she eventually died. Life was cheap then, for those who could not afford to live. What a travesty of human dignity, but all too often this indifference towards others less fortunate was something that happened—and unfortunately, continues.

Annie's Sisters

Mary Ann McDonald had three sisters—Susan, Betty, and Jessie—as well as three half-sisters and a brother. They were my mother's great-aunts. The youngest of the sisters, Susan, was married to a man called Charles Hill, who was the harbour master in Dundee's port. After he died, she went to live with her daughter, Betsy, who had married a vicar on the Lord Harewood estate in England. Susan had been spoiled for most of her life, and as a result, the two women often quarrelled; during such squabble, the mother would frequently pack all her belongings and return to Dundee, to Dallfield Walk. An important part of her transported luggage was the famous (or infamous) feathered quilt. Susan was 96 years old when she last appeared on the doorstep of the McElroys, but this time, the family had grown so she and her feathered quilt could not be accommodated. Susan was duly placed under the charge of the woman next door, who fortunately seemed to enjoy her company.

After a week or so, all were becoming a little irritated by the situation. Susan understood that she had to return to Betsy, her daughter. Unfortunately, Susan could neither read nor write, so she asked my mother if she would write to her daughter asking to return. With some persuasion in a second letter, Betsy agreed to her mother's return, but only on the expressed condition that her feathered quilt did not. It was to the great relief of the McElroy family, and the old lady next door, that old gran Susan, with great fuss and ceremony, left. After this traumatic ordeal, contact was lost, and it was only after the elapse of several years that the McElroy family learnt that Susan had died. So, she may well have reached her one hundredth birthday. I wish we knew.

The second daughter was Betty, and she married a McGregor who owned a bobbin and shuttle factory in the city. They had a son, who was given the fine Scottish name of Archie; they also had a daughter, and she was named after her aunt Susan. They lived for many years in a large house in City Road, close to their factory in Loons Road. Unfortunately, Betty had died during the birth of Archie, who because of this tragic delivery was brain damaged and suffered from severe learning difficulties for the rest of his life. Nevertheless, the whole family remained close, and he was cared for with great affection, particularly after the death of the father. Archie's aunt Jessie went to live in City Road as housekeeper and carer to the young man. The family business, which would have been inherited by Archie, was instead run by the daughters, Susan and Jessie. When Archie unfortunately died in his teens, they rightfully inherited the estate.

It may appear that this extended family of the McElroys was fated by tragedy and premature deaths, but this was typical of working-class people in the nineteenth and early twentieth centuries. Life was wrought with hardship and hazards. No one knew what the next day would bring, and it was lived from one payday (Friday) to the next.

A New Sister for Bessie

Nevertheless, Dallfield Walk, apart from a few unfortunate incidents, seemed to be a happy place where people went out of their way to help others—without too much imposed interference. During this time, Bessie recalled that her mother appeared to have one baby after another, and on each of these memorable occasions, she was told by her father to look out for the "Fifie boat." This was the paddle-driven ferryboat *(B. L. Nairn)* that crossed daily over the Tay, between Dundee's Craig Pier and Newport. It would bring the new baby across the river. So along with her brother, Jim, these two innocent souls would look out across the river towards Fife in expectation of the new arrival. Bessie was 6 years old before the next surviving addition to the family arrived; this was John. There then followed an interval of some four years before finally the youngest in the family safely came along; this was May. My mother now had a sister once again.

Nevertheless, there was a large age gap between the two sisters. Bessie was 14 years old and had been working for a full year before May first attended school. So, for many years, Bessie acted as a second mother to her sister. May, being by far the youngest sibling, was undoubtedly spoiled by the rest of the family, and this included Bessie. May followed her older sister almost everywhere, and of course, she was pampered and the recipient of small treats. Normally each Friday, young May would wait at the foot of the Hilltown for her sister returning from work, when she would receive two ounces of dolly-mixture sweets bought from Mr Brown's confectionary. Both sisters would then walk home hand in hand.

However, one Friday Bessie had not been paid, so she could not afford May's treat that day. When given the news, May looked at her sister with anger in her eyes and then walked away in silence. Bessie was hurt, and once home, she mentioned this to her mother, asking if anything was wrong. "No, nothing's wrang. That's just May. That lassie is just a law to herself" was the mother's reply. The following Friday, May was nowhere to be seen. In fact, she had found another source of sweetie supply and had abandoned her older sister. This was the start of other small, regrettable instances, and in time, a void was created between the two sisters, which never really healed. They remained respectful friends, but it took until their retiring years before they again started to associate like sisters. But even then, there was a hollowness in the relationship.

During a routine operation for a hip replacement, May, who by then was in her eighties, took a heart attack and died. For some unknown reason, the newspaper intimation of her death was delayed until after the funeral had taken place. Bessie, who by then was 91 years old, had been deprived of a final and lasting closure to her sister's death. Some five years on, when my mother died, there remained an openness of unanswered anxieties.

Bessie and May, Dallfield Walk. (Fife is seen in the background.)

In the Back Lands

Dundee had expanded rapidly during the previous century, although it was still relatively compact with high, dull, sandstone tenements (the result of the 1871 Dundee Improvement Act). To the east end of the present-day Victoria Road, which replaced the much narrower Bucklemaker Wynd, stood the Eagle Jute Mill with its iconic effigy of a giant eagle sitting aloft. Built in 1864 by the

Baxter brothers, this old mill is now divided into industrial units. Laced through these grey Victorian buildings were often much older and narrower cobbled streets that often intertwined into a complex of dark alleyways ("pends" or "closes"). The lower western end of Victoria Road, between Dallfield Walk and the tall, grey tenements of the lower Hilltown, now occupied by a massive multistorey block, there was a particularly dense maze of pends and backyards all interconnecting. Much of this dated back to the time when this area was called Bonnet-Hill, which was a throwback to bygone days when numerous bonnet makers (hatmakers) lived and worked in this area.

This Hilltown area was once part of the larger Dallfield estate that belonged to the Scrymgeour family, the one-time constables of Dundee. Although the tenants of this area were poor, they were regarded as decent, clean-living people. However, by the early twentieth century, these back lands had become a place of neglect. The neighbourhood was lit at night (if at all) by gaslight, which gave it an anxious air of sinister foreboding. Bessie remembered this as a dark and menacing place, particularly after a fall of rain, whereby a secret and sinister silence hung over the buildings. Dancing shadows from the gaslights created ghostly, misshapen figures against the crumbling grey walls of the alleyways. Through this dark backland, Bessie, now as a 14-year-old working woman, after a dance in the Progie Hall, which was in Norries Pend on the Hilltown, decided to walk home alone. She thought that this was the most direct and quickest route to Dallfield Walk.

That was a mistake.

So intent was she to return home at a reasonable time that she decided on this shortcut through the land of shadows and darkness. It was a relatively straight walk by daylight, but after a while in the dark gloom, she became disorientated, and a foreboding sense of fear slowly engulfed her into a state of almost panic. Bessie thought she heard someone. It was only a cat scurrying passed on its nightly prowl. Then something touched her face. It was only water dripping from a broken pipe. With fear gradually gripping her whole body, her heart started to thump. She sensed that someone was following, but it was the wind quipping up the puddles, producing leaping shadows all around. Bessie felt faint, and in blind terror she ran, splashing through mud-soaked puddles, through gaps in old, collapsed dykes, and along alleyways she had never seen before. Eventually, she had come full circle and reappeared back on the Hilltown, from Meekisons Close, where a young policeman found her bruised, bleeding, covered in mud, and crying. He took some convincing that nothing untoward had happened, but then he walked her home.

By now, her worried parents were anxiously looking out of their backroom window that overlooked Dallfield Walk. Steve already had his shoes on in preparation to search for his daughter, when she was spotted, strolling up the Walkie Brae without a care in the world, with her newfound policeman friend, whose name coincidentally happened to be Robert (or Bob). Nevertheless, Steve, thinking something drastic had happened, rushed downstairs to meet them. Bessie, on meeting her father in the street, and even more dire, her mother, who was glowering out of the window, cowered in silence behind Bob, allowing him to explain.

It transpired that she had told her parents that she was off to visit her girlfriend (another Mary) and would be home around ten o'clock and not to wait up, but the time was now well after eleven. However, she failed to mention that, in secret, she was dressed in her best clothes, hidden beneath her long coat. Also, Bessie had stealthily changed into her good shoes, which she had placed into the hallway (or lobby). Her friend Mary had done likewise; the girls then met and together hurried off to the weekly dance in the Progie Hall. This had been going on for some time, and they were confident that such a foolproof plan would not be discovered and could continue unknown to both sets of parents. Bessie knew that her father would be angry, but he was a "softy," and once the full story was told, he would forgive her. But her mother was a different "kettle of fish." From her, she expected a hard clout and a severe telling off, but to her amazement, she instead received a hug. Her mother then stood back and looked at her mud-caked, knee-bleeding, tearful daughter. There, she saw much of her own independent self and knew that a rebuke would be pointless. "Ah did the same at your age, but a managed no ti git covered in gutters or scart ma knees."[12] This was her mother's attempt at raw humour. She then changed her tone. "Well, yir a wurken lass noo, Bess, and yi ken yir ain mind, jist mak sure yir up fur yir work, at six."[13] Her mother then gave a slight impression of a smile. "Did yi hay a good time then, Bess?" "Eye, mither, I did" was the sheepish reply. And that was it. The dressing-down was over.

However, little did they know that Bessie and her friend Mary had been visiting the local dance halls for a whole year prior to this but had never told them. In fact, they never found out that part of the story. She knew that her parents would disapprove, so like most young people, despite it being just innocent fun, she kept it a secret. Where she was going and who she was going with were made up each week as Bessie left the house. Unknown to their parents, hiding their dance frock underneath their good coat had become a routine deception for these girls, and changing quickly into their cunningly hidden best shoes only added to the excitement. So, between the backroom of this small but-in-ben and the front door, Bessie changed from a little girl into a young woman, whereby she would dash off to the movies or to visit a friend, as her parent's thought.

During weekdays, the dancing ended early, so Bessie would reappear home at a reasonable time. She would then walk into the living room as innocent looking as she had left, having performed the reverse procedure in the lobby, as did Mary, her friend in crime. Parents did not worry so much about their children in those days. The streets were far safer, and it was a more respectful world than it is now. Street drunkenness and violence did not seem to be a great problem.

Both sets of parents realised that their respective daughters were becoming adults who not only knew their own mind but were

---

[12] "I did the same at your age, but I managed not to get covered in mud or scratch my knee."
[13] "Well, you're a working lass now, Bess, and you know your own mind. Just make sure you're up for your work at six."

prepared to take the consequences. Nevertheless, Bessie never took that so-called shortcut again, at least not at night. Steve became quite friendly with Robert, the beat policeman who received the affectionate nickname of "Bob the Bobby" from the family. To tease his daughter, Steve would often jokingly refer to Bob as Bessie's boyfriend. It always made her blush and giggle. As time went on, Bessie had her share of boyfriends and even a few offers of marriage, and that included Bob the Bobby, but she was not interested. The time was not right. She was too young and still preferred the dancing, but the main factor was her wage was needed by the family to make ends meet.

Voices in the Cupboard

As my grandfather Steve grew older, and as a direct result of the noise from the mill, he was afflicted by acute deafness; he still had an appreciating ear for music but could hear little else. This led to some weird situations that this elderly couple tended to drift into, and all played out in their small but-n-ben. My grandmother Mary told me that Steve often, in his favourite chair, sat looking out of their bedroom window, just watching the world go by, a pastime indulged in by many of the neighbours. They would chatter for hours on end with the other window-watchers on the opposite side of the street or with the passers-by below. In this way, they would keep up with local gossip and scandal, and there was always a scandal. Steve, of course, could not participate due to his deafness, but he would wave and nod to people below and generally enjoy the spectacle. In the main living room next door (the only other room in the house), and oblivious to Steve, was his wife hard at work. She had just completed washing some family items that were needed for the next day and was in the process of hanging them up. As it was a fine, sunny day, and due to the amount of washing involved, she decided to hang them outside. Normally, they were hung to dry on an inside pully system, referred to as a "horse." Every household had such a contraption that was attached to the ceiling. However, Gran, who by this time was in her seventies, climbed onto the coal bunker by the window and from there hung the clothes outside onto a rope system and tall, communal, wooden greenie pole. Once the task was complete, she then had to climb down from the bunker, but on this occasion, she stumbled, lost her balance, and fell straight into the large kitchen cupboard, the door of which then closed behind her. There was no room for manoeuvre so she could not open the door; she was trapped. It was pointless for her to call out due to Steve's deafness, so all she could do was wait.

Eventually, Steve came wandering through from the bedroom looking for his wife and of course could not find her. It was unlike Mary to leave the house without telling him. However, he could just hear her knocking but could not figure out where the noise was coming from. He shouted, "Whar ur ye, Mary?" Mary could not tell him for laughing; I am sure she stayed in the cupboard to see how long it took him to find her. When he eventually did open the cupbaord door, he casually remarked, "What ir yi dayin hiddin in the press fir, Mary?"[14] "A fell aff the bunker in nearly went through the wa ti the wifie's hoose nixt door."[15] Later, Steve jokingly said he thought his wife had gone a bit strange and wanted to play a game. Each time I visited my grandparents, they always had a weird or funny story to tell. They never failed.

I was only 11 years old when Steve died. I remember feeling so sorry for him, as he always seemed to be shouted at from my grandmother, but the man was deaf, so she had to be loud. My grandmother died at the age of 82 and my grandfather at 86, both stricken down by nothing more than old age due to a hard life. From the time they met, they loved each other dearly and were happy in each other's company. I suppose that's all that matters in life.

---

[14] "What are you doing hiding in the cupboard for, Mary?"
[15] "I fell off the bunker and nearly went through the wall to the woman's house next door."

Jock the Dog

It's strange how time can play tricks on one's memory and someone or something can so easily be forgotten but still play a very significant role in one's life. This was the case for my grandmother and Jock, the dog. As my grandparents grew older, they could always be found sitting side by side at the fireplace, reading. Lying alongside would be faithful Jock, raising his head each time they moved or spoke. He was a short-haired, black-and-white mongrel who literally followed Mary everywhere and was her perpetual friend.

On one memorable occasion, Mary led Jock into the back bedroom and locked him in so that she could spend time concentrating on her shopping in relative peace. However, the dog was so fond of her that he managed to prise open the window and scramble down to the street below. Mark you, they lived only one storey up on the first landing. He then ran all the way down Dallfield Walk in search of her.

I remember once standing in my uncle George's butcher shop (my father's brother), at the bottom of the Hilltown, when a dog unexpectedly appeared in the doorway. It scampered round the counter then out of the shop and up the hill. I looked at George, and he nodded. "Ah that's Jock," he said. "He's looking for your gran. He's away up the Hill to the bookshop now. That's where she'll be." Jock knew her routine; she would drop into George's shop for her butcher meat, cross the wide road at the bottom of the steep brae of the Hilltown, then continue walking up the hill, looking in every shop window on the way. On reaching the small second-hand bookshop, she would take some time browsing through dusty old pages that told of murder or love. There, Jock would meet her and then patiently sit waiting on his mistress making up her mind. A book for Steve would also be chosen; he liked murders and travel. Then the climb would continue, but this time in the company of Jock. The next stop would be the Plaza Cinema, where Mary always paused to look at the photographs displayed in the doorway of the picture house. The Plaza Cinema was an extremely plush affair with tall columns crowned by gilt-painted Corinthian capitals at the entrance. The staircase was enveloped in a thick carpet dotted with black and purple stars on a rich red background. The interior was every bit as luxurious with rows of lavish, upholstered seats, all fitted with the usual ashtrays. There were draped curtains hanging from each side of the silver screen, which was set back on a wide stage that gave the cinema an aura of the theatrical. Like so many Dundonians, Mary, accompanied by her daughter, Bessie, often attended the weekly performances, a moment of sheer luxury in the drab routine of working lives.

The bond between my grandmother and Jock continued for some fifteen years, until Mary died. Poor Jock, who had loved his mistress so much, had decided in his own way that he could not live without her. Within a week of her death, Jock had also gone.

CHAPTER 7

Young Bessie

Growing Up

During her primary schooling, young Bessie still had time to play her favourite game, which was dressing up. This was the influence from her aunt Maggie, who had so meticulously dressed her, and her older sister, Maria. During the long, dark evenings of winter when husband and wife would sit chatting beside a warm fire, Mary allowed her daughter, Bessie, to comb her long, pure, black hair. Despite the formidable reputation of the mother, there must have been a more placid and patient person behind her fearsome façade, as she allowed her daughter to busily arrange her hair in all sorts of different shapes. Another target for the artistic exploitations of Bessie's talent was the lady who lived next door. She lived on her own and would visit Mary most evenings just for a gossip, whereby she received similar treatment from this little girl. The women liked each other's company and would sit talking for hours over endless cups of tea, totally oblivious to the attentions of Bessie. Both women appeared to be completely unruffled as Bessie continued to play her games, whereby hats were then heaped, one upon the other, onto each adult's head.

In those days, there was much more interaction between the child and the parent, with more direct communication. There was no such thing as a generation gap or "teenager," that was an invention of the 1950s and 1960s. There were only people. Some were older, and some were younger (the little people), who were simply in the process of getting older, but all were expected to donate and play their optimum part in support of the family. The grandparents took care of the young grandchildren, while the parents worked. In turn, the young ones were sent out to work in the mills as soon as possible, thus contributing to the family's income and survival. In the early nineteenth century, young mothers often found it necessary to carry their babies into the factory, setting them to one side while they completed a full shift at the looms. In turn, these children, often as young as ten years, were expected to start their working lives. The Factory Act of 1833 prevented children under 9 years old to work in the mills, but 9-year-olds could. Girls, with their nimble fingers, were taught how to work the looms alongside their mother, and the boys, who did the heavier work, such as bagging the heavy spools of yarn, often worked with their fathers. The Factory Act of 1878 stopped child labour under 10 years. Later, these children could split their time, half of which was still in the mills, but now they could also attend school, where they received an elementary education (known as the "three Rs" of reading, writing, and arithmetic). Such children were known as the half-timers. Children who were attending school, or had attained a certain standard in education, could work part-time between the ages of 10 and 13. These half-timers were not regarded as children but as young persons; anyone over that age could work full-time, no matter their educational attainment. These requirements were of course not always adhered to by both sides: the employers who wanted cheap labour and the parents who needed the money.

Like my mother, my maternal grandmother was the eldest of the siblings. She had two sisters (Annie and Betsy) and three brothers (Charles, Albert, and Jack). Her mother, my maternal great-grandmother, was Anne Duthie McDonald, but Bessie referred to her as just Granny Donald. Her husband, John, had died relatively young, after which she moved into a small house in Rose Street to be closer to her sister. Each Sunday after chapel, Bessie would visit Granny Donald, which she looked forward to, as Aunt Annie and Uncle Albert were there. Annie always wore elegant and stylish clothes, which were mostly made by herself. Bessie wished that she were older and could thus wear clothes like those of her fashionable aunt, whom she deeply admired.

Annie later married, and she and new Uncle Jack, in due course, had a son named John. In 1919, just after the end of the Great War, when Bessie was 16 years old, Annie and her family emigrated to Wellington, New Zealand. There they settled, never to return to Dundee. Although migration to the far-off colonies of the British Empire was popular, it marked a final act of separation from both the old way of life and the rest of the family. But Bessie did not let go, keeping in touch by correspondence, so communication with her aunt Annie continued for several years.

Jack had been a seaman with the famous Dundee Whaling Fleet for most of his life, sailing the stormy Artic Ocean, but this did not prevent him from being seasick for most of the long voyage to the opposite side of the world. For the first time in his life, he was not part of the working crew; he was a passenger with time on his hands—time to be unsettled by the sea. On the other hand, his wife and young son enjoyed a very pleasant and relatively uneventful sea journey. Jack had saved the enormous sum of £300, enough to buy a small bungalow on the outskirts of Wellington, and thus became firmly settled on dry land. He found work as a docker in the port of Wellington; this was as close to the sea as he was ever again likely to get. Being a docker, loading and unloading cargo vessels, was hard and dangerous, but the pay was good and there was plenty of work.

According to the letters arriving home to Bessie, the whole family was well and prospering. However, like so often, tragedy strikes suddenly at human affairs and ruthlessly takes its toll. Jack unfortunately found himself in the wrong place at the wrong time during one of his shifts at the dockside. A winch attached to one of the unloading cranes snapped. The crane buckled and collapsed onto the key side at the exact spot where Jack was working; he was killed instantly.

If the loss of a husband was not enough, fate again struck Annie with another equally devastating blow. Not long after Jack's death, her son, John, fell prey to tragic misfortune. By then he was a man of twenty and had become a state warden in an open prison. On horseback he covered his area of responsibility, and it was at the start of one such tour of duty that he was bitten by an insect. He had been bitten before, so thinking nothing about it, he completed his shift without treatment. It was too late. The infection had set in, from which he never recovered, dying a week later. Annie, no longer a young woman, had lost her entire family and was alone. From a new life in a new world, fate had dealt her a cruel blow, and what had started as a future full of dreams with so much hope had gone. She had to start again in another direction, on her own.

Annie was at heart a Dundee woman, strong and able, so she fell back on her own skills and resources. She had always been outstanding at knitting and crotchet work, so that's what she did. At first, Annie sold her products locally, but in time this expanded and developed into a successful cottage industry. Despite the frustrations, blows, and disappointments that life had thrown her way, this widowed woman had done well. My mother had followed Annie's life through correspondence, becoming her close confidante and pen pal. Annie lived out the rest of her days, in relative comfort, in her adopted country of New Zealand. Life is strange. It is what you and no one else make of it, and Annie made the most of it.

My mother was named after her second aunt, Betsy, who remained in Dundee. She married an agreeable, good-natured man called Tom Henry, and like my grandfather, left most of the family affairs in the capable hands of his wife. They had a son, Tom, named after his father, and a daughter, Annie, named after her aunt. This family also experienced misfortune as Betsy was tragically killed while crossing Victoria Road at the city's Meadow Side junction. I at the time was around 5 years old and remember sharing the experience of loss that the family felt. It also evoked a realisation in me that no matter the nature of the loss, whether it be on a far-off battlefield, a mere insect bite, or this, a local road accident, the same sense of bereavement is felt. It was certainly a loss from which her husband, Tom, never recovered.

Following the traditional footsteps of many Dundee men, and to the disdain of much of the family, Bessie's uncle Charles became a whaler. It was a dangerous way of life, away from his family for months on end, and then often his time at home was short before he was off to sea again. He married a jute worker (a spinner) called Betty, and my mother clearly recalled their wedding day; in fact, as a young 8-year-old schoolgirl, it was one of her most vivid and lasting memories. It was the first wedding she had ever attended and had never been so close to a bride. She thought Betty was the most beautiful person she had ever seen, in her white wedding vail with long, golden hair waving in a light breeze. The bride was so happy that day.

The couple had two daughters and for many years lived a contented life. Alas, things could not last, and poor Charles was drowned in the Bay of Biscay in 1914, just at the start of the Great War. Some members of the family claimed he had been torpedoed; others said that he was washed overboard and struck by the ship's propeller, which I think would have been unlikely considering his whaling experience. Sudden death and tragedy were commonplace in those days, whereby the surviving husband or wife simply had to accept their predicament of fate, rearrange their life, and continue. Betty was luckier than most widows. She received compensation and opened a small shop, and in this way, she continued to survive. It's just as well we don't know what lies ahead of us.

Bessie's uncle Albert could have been considered one of the lucky ones, as he managed to survive the Dardanelles Campaign during the Great War and was regarded by the family as a hero. The Dardanelles Campaign between the Ottoman Empire and the Western allies (France and Britain) was designed to eliminate Turkish support for Germany and shorten the war. However, the Ottomans proved to be much tougher than expected, and due to mismanagement of the campaign, the whole struggle spectacularly backfired. The British withdrew, and Albert's regiment was sent back to the Western Front.

On his return, he rented a flat in Blackness Road, and for a while, he entered the grocery trade, but the time he had spent fighting abroad had taken its toll and more damage had been done to this man than anyone realised at the time. He was only in his fifties when he apparently gave up on life and just died. Many young men of that generation were never the same on their return home; they never managed to settle. This had been a world war so similar disorders applied to the soldiers of the other countries involved. The Great War was followed by the Great Depression (1929—1939) and worldwide discontent; it is little wonder that the Second World War ensued scarcely two decades after the first. My father always claimed that the Second War was only a continuation of the first; after all, it was only the armistice that stopped the fighting, followed by a twenty-year gap that enabled Germany to recoup and resume. He would say, "If you're going to the trouble of fighting a war, then make sure that the winners don't become the losers."

The Movies

It was during my mother's early days that silent movies first appeared; this was the start of the picture house era, and cinemas sprang up all over town. Bessie took my grandmother to see her first silent movie in the Plaza Cinema on the Hilltown. Seemingly, my gran sat in astonished amazement just staring at the screen in disbelief. From then on, she attended the cinema regularly, no matter what was showing. Although the whole family knew that she never quite came to terms with moving pictures, she would turn up at the Plaza door, long before opening time, always escorted by one of the family. And whosoever accompanied her knew to say absolutely nothing, not a single word, throughout the entire performance; the silence was broken only by the complementary music of a single piano played live below the screen. Also, during evening performances, Bessie often accompanied her father after his work to the Plaza. He would pay the grand total of two-pence each for the best circle seats. There, her father would quietly sit, totally mesmerised, no matter what was showing.

Another cinema close by was the Empire Theatre in Rosebank Street, and each Saturday morning, Bessie and her brother Jim would queue with their friends outside for the children's movie matinee. On entry into the cinema, which only cost one penny, the children were each supplied with either an apple or an orange. Once inside, and despite the movies being silent, the matinees were anything but. Between the noise of the children and the pianist attempting to play over them, the hall was in an uproarious state of pandemonium. Normally, there were two films with a half-hour intermission between them, during which time they were permitted to eat their fruit. Also, in this period, the audience could participate in the "Go as you please competition." Here, anyone could take part by simply climbing onto the stage and waiting until you were called to perform. There was one certainty: no matter how good or bad the performers were, they were always guaranteed a rowdy reception. The audience would then cheer for the act they liked best, and the winner received a prize. Once among all the confusion and noise, little Jim suddenly appeared on stage and volunteered to sing the "Blue Ridge Mountains of Virginia," which had been a Laurel and Hardy song and was sung regularly as a duet by both Bessie and Jim. During Jim's performance, he forgot the words, but Bessie shouted at the top of her voice the rest of the song from the front of the audience. She then climbed onto the stage beside her brother, and both gave an encore. They jointly won first prize, which on that morning happened to be an old homemade magic lantern, and together they proudly carried their prize, along with some slides, home to show the family.

A magic lantern was the forerunner of the film projector, and the DVD unit, where complicated electronics replaced a simple candle. This candle was placed inside the lantern, and through a small hole and lens, a light was projected onto a makeshift screen, or simply the living room wall. The slides were then projected and focused. My grandmother was not all too impressed by this gadget, as she did not know what it was, but Steve soon had it cleaned and working. For a long time, it became the centrepiece of family entertainment and many a long winter's night was spent watching the slides and creating their own animations. As far as the children were concerned, it was magic. No one recalls what happened to the lantern. It seemed to just disappear, like magic. Probably the family outgrew yesteryear's entertainment, and it was set aside as a pleasant memory of their childhood.

While still on the theme of entertainment, each Saturday morning Bessie would receive a threepenny piece (two-and-a-half pence) from her mother. This would pay for her and her brother into the matinee with a penny left over for sweets. She recalled that on one Saturday, while standing in the queue and moving closer to the Empire Theatre doors, Bessie put her hand into her pocket for the threepenny piece, but it had gone. She had lost the money and started to cry. Now as this tragedy was unfolding at the entrance to the cinema, a wee lad standing next to them in the queue said that his friend had found a threepenny piece in Rosebank Road. It must have been the lost coin. Who else could it have belonged to but Bessie? As far as she was concerned, it was her money, and she immediately instigated a search to find this poor innocent boy.

By this time, the little boy was also in the queue, and Bessie immediately descended upon him, but he refused to part with the money. He was then reported to the doorman, who sided with Bessie, but still he refused, at which point he was thrown out of the queue and banned from entry into the cinema for a month. This was a serious situation and the boy by then was in floods of tears as he was sent away in shame from the queue, but he still held the threepenny piece tightly in his hand. Bessie and Jim were then allowed into the cinema free of charge.

On their arrival home, this was related with great enthusiasm to their mother, and the picture they painted of the denounced villain was by no means complimentary. It was not until the next Monday morning while preparing for school that Bessie felt something in the lining of her coat and guess what popped out. Yes, it was the threepenny piece. It had been there all the time after slipping through a hole in the pocket. Guilt, horror, and fear poured through Bessie, all at the same time. Her mind raced. She could not possibly tell her mother, having made such a song and dance about the whole episode in the first place. It was also the best way to get a clout, so that was not an option. Also, this small boy had been accused of stealing, it went through Bessie's young mind that he may be stigmatised for the rest of his life, and it was all her fault. She had never seen him before and didn't know who he was. Probably he was a Protestant, and that was why she did not know him, and they would never meet again. What was Bessie to do? This all went on in her mind for days, during which time she held onto the money. Her conscience, however, relented with time, and she and her brother decided to spend the ill-gotten proceeds, but in secret. After all, the boy still had the threepenny piece that he had found. I wonder who really lost the money.

It seemed an age before all the money was spent. They cunningly bought sweets and candy apples in dribs and drabs so as not to be noticed. Bessie bought extra pencils and a slate for the school; above all, it was her who found the money in her coat. Their parents never found out, and Bessie did not find the boy who had been so unceremoniously ejected from the cinema queue at her instigation. Even in her old age, I could see a distant tinge of guilt hidden behind her smiling eyes.

Incident Prone

Working people, although underprivileged and poor, were very proud, especially the women, who tried as best they could to keep their families and homes as clean and tidy as possible. This conscious pride in respectability extended to visiting personages that included such people as the doctor, the church elder, and even the rent man. On such occasions, the women would fuss around the house, cleaning and sweeping up. Finally, they would put on a clean apron (or pinny), just before the expected arrival, and then pretend that everything in this poor but now spotless house was part of their everyday norm.

Bessie's induction into assuming the second mother in the family was rapid, whereby she became just as fussy and house proud as her mother. It may have appeared that Mary was less protective of her eldest sibling, and she certainly could never have been described as overprotective towards her, but she did worry and with good reason, where Bessie was concerned. She was the most accident-prone member of the family. Her mother claimed that if anything were to happen, it would happen to Bessie.

Of all the tales that Mary would frequently tell, she always included the poker incident, which was almost a major tragedy in the family, so this was told with great passion and drama with a tear in her eyes. Bessie, being the oldest, was responsible for certain chores around the house. One such chore that was expected of her was to set the coal fire in preparation for the evening. On arrival from school each day, she would rake the hearth of ash and cinders from the previous night. The cinders were reused by wrapping them up in a few sheets of old newspaper. This was placed to one side; the rest of the newspaper sheets were then rolled up and tied into knots and placed neatly in the hearth. Sticks followed on top, then coal. The wrapped cinders then topped it all. Bessie did not have permission to ignite the paper before her parents arrived home from work, but on this fateful occasion, due to the cold and wintery weather, she did. The house was fine and warm on their arrival, so nothing was said, and they settled down before the start of the evening meal.

To allow air into the fire and so kindle quicker, a poker was partially pushed into its centre. It was only a moment or two later that Bessie remembered that the poker was still there. She stretched out to retrieve it from the hearth, not realising that the heat from the fire had passed along the length of the metal. Her screams were heard on the other side of Dallfield Walk as her small fingers burnt against the metal. She told me that she could still feel and hear the skin on her fingers and hand sizzle and crack. She instinctively tried to pull her hand away, but the poker stuck to it like burning glue. She started to panic and tried to knock the poker away, but the red-hot poker stuck to these fingers as well. She went into shock. Her mother could only cry out, "Oh my bairn, help her," which she cried out again and again. At the same time, her father, Steve, sprang to his feet and dragged his daughter to the sink, where he turned on the tap water as hard as possible over her hands and poker. Steam filled the room, and after what they thought was an age, the poker separated from the hands and fell into the sink. Bessie was unconscious, but Steve sprinted with her in his arms all the way to their doctor's surgery.

This was Dr Wenjon, whose practice was at the bottom of Constitution Brae, scarcely a half mile away. The quick action of my grandfather saved my mother's fingers and perhaps her life. She said she could remember nothing but pain that night, and for weeks after. With both hands bandaged, she could do absolutely nothing for herself. In many ways, Bessie had been extremely lucky, although her fingers bore the scars of that night for the rest of her life.

The family had also been traumatised; and it was during this period of recuperation and convalescence that her mother displayed the caring and tender side towards her daughter. Bessie said that she never felt as close to her mother as she did then. From then on, even during phases of extreme scolding, Bessie saw the compassionate side of a concerned mother radiating through, something she had never recognised in her mother but nevertheless had always been there. Bessie had learnt the hard way, and until her marriage, she never set another fire.

A School Incident

My grandparents complemented each other's contrasting characteristics; they were both ardent readers and aware of most current events. Whether at a local, national, or international level, little passed them by. Steve was the more placid in nature but with a strong, determined streak when necessary. This was especially true when the well-being of the family was at stake. He was not only clever but also a kind man who was loved and respected by his family. Mary, on the other hand, was a more formidable person who tended to flare up more so than Steve but would then calm down just as quickly. However, Mary's formidable nature was displayed on one memorable occasion while Bessie was still in her primary years at school.

A nun/teacher (Sister Maria) for some unknown reason took a terrible dislike to Bessie. She would pick on and blame her for almost anything that went wrong in class. One day while conducting a music lesson, the nun attempted to hit a high note and her voice suddenly became throaty and hoarse. The class was expected to sit still and pretend that nothing untoward had happened, which they did. But when it happened a second time, the girl sitting directly behind my mother (Mary Leishman) could not contain herself any longer and released a single loud burst of laughter. The whole class then started to quietly giggle. That was enough as far as Sister Maria was concerned. Completely enraged, she demanded that Bessie step forward, but my mother thought that she meant the real culprit, Mary, who was sitting behind, and so she remained seated. The nun raced towards the wrong pupil, gripped her hair, and dragged Bessie to the front of the class. Now in those days and especially in Forebank School, for a young Catholic child to be on the wrong side of, and chastised by, an angry nun was one of the most terrifying experiences imaginable. In sheer terror, Bessie froze, and this memory was instantly and indelibly stamped into her mind for ever. Despite a few protests from some brave pupils, she was caned for the first time in her life, and to make things worse this was in front of the whole class. To Bessie, even the thought of being struck by this long, thin stick was inconceivable, but it had happened. Punishment by caning was not only severe, but the humiliating manner by which it was delivered was demeaning. During the execution of this punishment, the cane would whistle through the air on its journey to the recipient's open hand, often landing inaccurately, and large bruises would then appear on their wrist and arm. In Bessie's case, the delivery was bad and the cane crashed down onto her wrist. The shock was stunning; she had never been struck like that before—or after. She had always been an ideal pupil, did well at her lessons, and was quiet in class. It was not so much the pain, and my mother knew what real pain felt like. That was bad enough. It was the speed at which the entire incident took place and the injustice of it all. In retrospect, she always felt anger at the unfairness of being punished for something she was totally innocent of. Bessie never mentioned the incident to her mother, but it was brought to her attention through the neighbourhood grapevine, and she was furious. To Bessie's surprise, this fury was not directed at her, which she was afraid of, but towards the offending nun, and her mother was a match for any over authoritative nun.

Parents did not approach, far less reproach, authority, and that included the school. This was the case particularly for Catholic families, where the school system not only held great sway over the child's education but also influenced the whole family. Despite being aware of the frustrations that some nuns and priests took out on their charge, parents normally said nothing. These parents had often experienced similar bullying in their youth, but the working-class mentality of the time meant that they *knew their place* and were not prepared to interfere. Frequently, first thing on Monday morning, it was not unusual for a priest to ask a child at random the colour of his Sunday mass vestment. If the child did not know, or could not remember, it was assumed that they were absent from Sunday mass so caned. The caned child, more times than not, was afraid to report the incident back home for fear that they would receive another hard clout from one of their parents. Parents just did not want to know; it was easier to blame the child rather than stand up to prejudicial authority, and the school was the authority, albeit under the umbrella of the Catholic Church.

For the most part, this was the attitude of my grandparents, but this time things had gone too far. My grandmother had been a Protestant who converted to Catholicism and was therefore not overawed by her adopted church. She did not impart the same demanding reverence that it received from the rest of the devout family. So next day, off she marched to the school, with Bessie timidly tagging on behind, wishing that the ground would open and swallow her. The nun involved would not face Mary, but the priest did, and initially he even talked down to her. That was a mistake. She was not to be intimidated by any arrogant, patronising priest; all hell let loose. Eventually, in a futile attempt to appease her, he held up in her face the cross that hung round his neck. He was lucky she didn't strangle him with it. "Never mind hiding behind the cross!" she shouted in a clear but determined voice that bellowed through the corridors of the school. "You're no man of God! You, nor yours, will ever strike my daughter like that again." And it worked. At school, Bessie was never bullied or harassed by any nun or priest again, as that was exactly what it was. In fact, she went on to win many prizes at school, especially for essay writing.

There are instances in life that unwittingly colour one's perceptive judgement, and this was one. Forebank School was a place where she allowed her imagination to excel, but despite this affectionate esteem for learning, her perception of Catholicism had changed, and not for the better.

Bessie's Education

My mother was 5 years old when she started to attend Forebank Primary School. The moved from Patterson Street to Dallfield Walk was a bonus for Bessie as it meant that she was now closer to her school. This was of far more importance than acting as nursemaid to a mere younger brother, Jim. Bessie, young though she was, felt that her schooling was paramount, and she became engrossed in all that was about her, wanting to know everything about everything. She became literate early in life, spelling being her forte. And like my grandparents, she was an ardent reader, which became one of the most important factors in her long life. My grandmother Mary, although reasonably well educated, was more vocal and tended to express herself more so than the rest of the family, so she often dominated domestic affairs, which apparently suited Steve and the rest, including Bessie, who would often quietly sit, reading, while about her were the usual turmoil and noise of family life. Sometimes mayhem would erupt, but still she sat oblivious to her surroundings. The recipient of a sudden clout around the ear would bring her back into family life, whereby she would quickly respond and adhere to the voiced demand of her mother, before getting back to her reading. From what I can remember, my grandfather and mother were the scholars in the family.

During Bessie's young primary school days, she rushed home each afternoon; her mother, Mary, would be found sitting with the young family, all waiting on her return. They would sit round the fireside singing the old songs, which included the nursery rhymes "The Farmer's in His Den," "Wee Willie Winkie," and "Hickory Dickory Dock." Her young brother, Jim, loved hearing the riddle.

> "A wee, wee man
> In a red, red coat,
> A stick in his hand
> And a stone in his throat.
> Who am I?"

Of course, the answer was always the same, and Jim would shout it out as loud as he could. "A cherry!" At the age of 96, my mother said that she could still clearly hear their voices, and in such detail, as if it were only yesterday.

Mary would then rise to prepare the evening meal in time for the father's arrival from work. While this was happening, Bessie looked after the rest of the family. She would arrange them into a pretend classroom, and of course Bessie would be their teacher. The lesson was about things she had learnt that day in class. Even at that early age, her ambition was to be a teacher, but life does not grant all that one may desire, and this was not to be. She said that she never regretted any part of her life. After all, her two sons did become teachers. She believed that throughout life there were many different paths that could be followed. Some are followed and explored, but most are not, only being left to one's imagination as to what could have been. The path that was followed by my mother was made as interesting, colourful, and full of life as she could possibly make it, and nothing more. Happy with that, she had no regrets.

Nevertheless, by marrying into a Protestant family, Bessie had swapped religious camps, but my mother's heart probably always remained Catholic. This was despite her two sons being brought up as loyal Protestants. Her belief was more towards a more moderate Catholic Church, and this became patently clear close to the end of her life. However, she always maintained a tarnished view of many of its minions, including the pent-up aggression of some nuns, but at the same time remembered the kindness and patience of others. Never did she regret her marriage to Sandy and her shift in loyalties, saying that it allowed her to see that God saw people, not just Catholics.

The Ivory Brooch

Bessie, despite her setback, continued with her own personal enlightenment all through her life; she read as much as possible, not only the current literature of the day but also the works of the great authors. Bessie often mentioned her admiration for such people, who had the ability to put feeling into words and describe so ingeniously what they saw in their mind's eye. While reading, this young girl would have as her constant companion a dictionary, to which she frequently referred.

So, despite any nun-like venom, her love for reading and especially essay writing never diminished. Anything that fired her fertile imagination became the theme of her next essay. Around 10 years old, she recalled one such composition. In it, Bessie had made herself the subject, whereby she pretended to be an ivory brooch that was once part of the tusk of an African elephant. This was a time when hunting and killing of wild animals was a favoured pastime among the classes of the colonial elite, with little regard for the animals that were shot or the ecosystem they lived in. In Africa, the brooch was sold to a missionary lady who then travelled home to Scotland. Bessie, as the brooch, then found herself living in a large country house in the Scottish Highlands and pinned to a beautiful fur coat, which in those days would certainly have been from a real animal. Unfortunately, after a few adventures in the Highlands, the brooch pin became loose and fell from the coat's lapel into a babbling brook on the west coast of the country, whereupon it was washed out to sea. Here, in the depth of the ocean, Bessie was swallowed up by a large, hungry fish. Many years went by, and after the fish had travelled the seven seas, it found itself once again off the coast of Africa, where it was caught in the net of a fisherman.

In the meantime, the same rich lady had returned to her African missionary. On the last day of her visit, she decided to do her own shopping and in the local market purchased a large, fine-looking fish, which was then presented to the kitchen staff ready for gutting and cooking. Under the watchful eye of the lady, the cook's sharp knife cut into the belly of the fish and guess what popped out. That's right, Bessie. Some "tail," for a 10-year-old child.

Lost Dreams

By the age of 13, Bessie had won a bursary, mainly for her essay writing, which would have allowed her to continue her education, eventually entering the convent teaching academy. Her ambition was to become a teacher, and it appeared that all was going to plan. But the war was still raging, and victory was nowhere in sight. In fact, we seemed to be losing. On the home front, conditions were not good, and all available resources were for the war effort. Hence, the bursary was worth only £5 per year and was meant to cover books and clothing; living expenses were not even considered. Her father had been employed in a luxury trade (a carpetmaker), so for most of the war, and for a long time after, he was idle. To add to the dilemma, her mother was again pregnant. The whole system was against Bessie, and at the age when she should have started her vocational dream, it turned into a nightmare. What she had wanted most in her life seemed to be slipping from her grasp. The priests pleaded with her parents that their daughter be given this chance to continue with her studies, but the unadorned truth was they could not afford to let her go. It was not their fault; they both knew the importance of a good education and how much it meant to Bessie. The culprit was the time in which they lived.

This conflict between her dreams and duty placed great stress on my mother, but what else could she do? She was the eldest sibling in the family and obliged to work and help bring up the rest of the siblings. Her father, Steve, was heartbroken as he realised that a talent was being lost, but I always remember being told that her mother, Mary, was somewhat relieved when things were finally settled. A more practical person than Steve, she did not want to stretch beyond her station; she knew her place in life. Mary felt that the eldest sibling in the family, especially if it was a female, was expendable. Bessie fitted both categories, so her ambition was set aside. At the age of 13, she left school and started full-time work among the dust and noise of the Dundee jute mills.

Starting work so young in the mills was the norm in those days, and there was little else for any Dundee girl leaving school. There was no choice, and if Bessie could not carry on with her studies, then by earning as much as she could for the family, her sacrifice may after all have been worthwhile. Little though her weekly wage was, she agreed to hand it all over to her mother while her father was idle—and a few years later while her younger brother Jim completed his apprenticeship as a painter. My grandparents, especially my grandmother, felt that they had enough worries on their plate without the added anxiety of their daughter's education. Bessie's feelings were secondary when it came to the welfare and survival of the whole family. It was better to have a family income based on two wages each week than one. Small though her wage may have been, it was needed.

However, when the time came for John (the younger of the brothers) to leave Forebank School, there was no problem, although it was now too late for Bessie. John certainly was not the brightest in the family, but he was bright enough to hold a job in the jute factories and earn a higher wage than an apprentice, so his fate was decided quickly. Personally, I remember John as an extremely good-natured person. He was enthusiastic—*fanatical*—about football. As a young man, he played a few games as goalkeeper for the Arbroath Football Club. For a long time, it appeared that football was all that mattered to him. If only Jim had been more like his younger brother John, then Bessie may have been given the chance of achieving her dream of becoming a teacher.

Of course, things have changed since then, and daughters are no longer expected to make such a sacrifice, as is any other sibling. Families now tend to be more heterogeneous than in the past, whereby daughters can express themselves more openly and be equally independent. All family members are now free to pursue their own dreams and aspirations. Thank goodness.

Uncle Albert

My mother was around 11 years of age when the First World War broke out in 1914, and by that time, she was starting to develop a very fertile imagination. She had started to study French at school, and this helped her with place names in France and their pronunciation. Along with her literary skills, this helped her follow the progress of the war until the armistice of 1918. French names and places became quite familiar to her as she read the newspaper articles and studied the limited maps and the battle campaigns that were released to the public. Such press releases were of course heavily censored, but they did give her an indication of how the war was going. Her youthful immaturity allowed her never to doubt, at any time, who the ultimate victors would be, far less question the moral grounds upon which the war was fought.

Her uncle Albert was one of the early conscripts into the army, and by 1915, he had been shipped off to Gallipoli and into the disastrous

Dardanelles conflict. He was the youngest of her uncles and only 19 when he was called up. Albert had a lively sense of humour and astute sharp wit. He was Bessie's favourite uncle, and she dutifully wrote to him throughout the entire war, telling him about the news back home and local gossip. During the war, all schoolchildren were encouraged to write to the soldiers at the front, and Bessie's letters to her uncle Albert won many prizes, which of course, encouraged her to write even more. But the war had done something to Uncle Albert, and the entertaining, lovable young man who had left Dundee was not the same man who returned.

Bessie vividly remembered her uncle's return home. He was still only 25 years old, and Bessie 16, but he had lost his youth. She recalled their first meeting after almost five years; it was in their house on Dallfield Walk. She was so excited that she ran nonstop from the west end of the town, where she was working, all the way home to meet him. He was sitting in the front room with his back to the door, so at first glance, she could not see his face. Her mother, Mary, smiled gently at her and then turned to her brother. "Albert, there's someone here to see you." As Albert turned towards Bessie, her heart almost stopped. She was looking at an old man.

My mother was always able to compose herself, and she quickly recovered from the shock, but her eyes filled with tears when he asked who she was. "This is Bessie, your young niece," Mary said in an unfamiliar soft and compassionate voice. Bessie could not speak as they simply just shook hands.

Sitting on the edge of the settee, my mother had been stunned at what the war, which she had followed with so much enthusiasm, had done to her favourite uncle. Although she had seen men return from France minus limbs, often blind and disfigured, her young mind could not fully comprehend what had happened. She knew that some soldiers suffered from a condition known as shell shock, which caused balance problems, paralysis of certain limbs, and even the loss of coordinated speech, but surely not Uncle Albert. She vividly remembered a neighbour, Mrs Brown, whose three handsome sons fell victim to the war. The first was blown to pieces by a landmine, the second had a leg amputated, and the third spent the rest of his life in a mental institute (or asylum) due to shell shock. Bessie often wondered what went on in Mrs Brown's mind as she sat at her window day after day, nursing her broken heart, another victim of the war. As she looked out and saw the depravation and poverty that followed the 1918 armistice, she must have queried what had been won; was all this suffering worthwhile? This same question was undoubtedly raised by the surviving soldiers on their return to what? A land fit for heroes?

Despite all that was inflicted upon these poor people during the war, most rejected hearing the truth, preferring to exist in a world of denial. The public had become immune to any unofficial adverse reporting and was conditioned to believe only the watered-down hype from government sources. Even when the lists of dead and missing were posted in the city, after the Battle of Loos in 1915, where thousands of local Black Watch soldiers had died in the mud of France, people chose to insulate themselves, believing the official line of propaganda, which promoted honour and duty. They did not know that almost 60,000 British and Allied forces were killed at Loos, of which almost all officers and many Dundee men of the Fourth Black Watch died. Out of the 30,000 Scots who fought in this battle, 7,000 were killed, almost one in every four, not to mention the thousands wounded and those taken prisoner.

But Albert's condition was real. The powers to be had destroyed this lovely man, and there was nothing honourable in that. From that moment on, Bessie regarded the Great War as an unnecessary evil act of shame that contained no noble cause, glory, or glamour; it was simply the end product in the lust for greed and power by a small minority of world leaders—irrespective of consequences.

In the years to come, the truth of the war gradually seeped through, mainly from returning soldiers. They were ordinary working people (on both sides) who had been subjected to the gore of dehumanising conditions in the trenches of the frontline. Through her reading of news articles and word of mouth from convalescing soldiers, Bessie knew something of what was happening, but neither she nor anyone at home understood the full extent of the bloodletting carnage that went on during this slaughter. There had never been such wholesale butchery in the history of humankind, and to the Western world's ignominy, it was fought almost entirely on European soil, at the instigation of Christian countries. Yet the lesson was not learnt. Nevertheless, little did they know what still lay ahead.

Bessie had been working for three years when her uncle returned. He still thought of her as an 11-year-old schoolgirl with ribbons in her hair. He, like so many young men, had lost his youth and things were not as he remembered. Still only in his early twenties, but with all he had seen and been through, Albert had a much older head on his young shoulders. Also, with hundreds of demobbed soldiers pouring back into the city, finding a job only added to his problems. It took him a long time to readapt and fit back into a civilian routine (if he ever did).

My mother had always called him "Uncle Abbie." That was fine in private, but he insisted that in public she dropped the title of uncle. "Albert" was enough. He felt that strangers would think that he was much older than he was if they knew he had a 16-year-old niece. He explained, "It makes me feel like an auld man." Bessie did not mind this and respected his wishes. In fact, she regarded it as a compliment, recognising that she was now a grown woman. However, on one occasion she did forget and did spectacularly violate this agreement. It was one Sunday afternoon as Bessie with a few girlfriends was walking along the old Overgate, a long, narrow street in the centre of town filled with an array of shops, amusements, and a market. On the opposite side was a group of young men, Albert being one of them; they were obviously eyeing up the girls. Nevertheless, this ongoing situation was almost ruined when Bessie saw her uncle and blared out, and she had a loud voice, "Hello, Uncle Abbie!" There was no response, so Bessie repeated her greeting with an even greater volume of enthusiasm. At the time, she wondered why he gave her just a wee smile and a half wave. One of the men jokingly called over, "Are you Abbie's sister?" She replied, "No, I'm his young niece." Bessie then remembered their agreement, and in a vain attempt to put things right, she only made them worse. "Oh! Sorry, Uncle Abbie. I mean Albert. Oh, I forgot." To Albert, things were deteriorating into nothing more than a disaster, but the two groups saw the funny side and they started to talk and intermingle. Soon Uncle Abbie had forgotten his embarrassment. He gave Bessie a cuddle and started to joke and be his old familiar self. The girls were all treated to an ice cream, and together the group walked along the Overgate and back. In later years, this became Dundee's famous "Monkey Walk," and it was where the young people met and mixed. These men had all been in the war and had all been in some way affected by it.

It was then that Abbie explained to his niece that her letters meant so much to him during the Dardanelles Campaign and that they kept him in touch with home and reality. He had tried to put the war behind him and be the man he once was, but the memory of killing and lost comrades made that impossible. He once said that it was the smell of death that lingered mostly in his mind and memory; the war never really left him. Poor Abbie survived until his early fifties when he contracted tuberculosis and shortly thereafter died. The whole family regarded him with great affection, and they would often during the long winter nights, while huddled round the fireplace in their small, gas-lit room, recall his memory. Later, my mother would tell her own family about that meeting in Dundee's Overgate. It was important to her, as in that group of young men, and little known to her at the time, was a man called Sandy, her future husband.

Dr Wenjon

During the Great War, Dallfield Walk remained a close community, where its people quickly rallied round to help each other. This was the case during times of unemployment, illness, and bereavement. Such neighbourliness was particularly tested as the war came to an end and returning soldiers brought home the influenza pandemic of 1918 (or Spanish flu). The whole country was stricken, and it was totally indiscriminate, affecting the young and the old alike, the healthy along with the frail. All were vulnerable to this strain of flu. Worldwide, it was reckoned to have claimed 100 million lives, which made it probably the deadliest of all recorded disasters in human history, perhaps a display of God's wrath for our stupidity in waging war.

My grandmother, who was always willing to help her neighbours, continually moved in and out of the houses affected. This did nothing to stem the spread of the virus, but help was required, so she attended anyone who needed her, always taking with her a pot of homemade broth. This was always on the boil, and she made so much that many mothers would send their youngsters to her door for a flagon of the broth. On the same tenement landing as my grandparents lived two spinster sisters, and both went down with the virus. They were looked after and supplied with a flagon of broth each day, but it was Bessie who ran for their daily shopping and generally attended to them. The result was that she also caught Spanish flu. As the infection took hold, she had to leave her work and take to her bed, and as the symptoms got worse, her hair started to fall out until she was completely bald, except for a small tuft that remained at the back of her head. This was devastating for a 16-year-old girl, but the family doctor (Dr Wenjon) assured her that it would all grow back. This tuft of hair was a source of great amusement for the rest of the family, and her aunt Betsy would flick it each time she passed. This certainly did not amuse the patient. Dr Wenjon of course was correct, and her hair did grow back, and with a vengeance, thicker and darker than it had ever been and full of curls. Her friends thought it was a wig and would not believe that the hair was real until they had given it a good hard pull.

My mother described Dr Wenjon as a "jewel of a man" who had helped her through burnt fingers, the great flu pandemic, and a bald head. He was also regarded as a family friend by most of his registered patients. He was a very caring individual, and for those who could not afford expensive doctor's bills, he simply did not send one, depending on the honesty of his patients to eventually pay something when they could. Of course, some patients would never pay, but most did. On occasions when my grandmother had the money, she would send Bessie along to his surgery with a half crown (25p) in advance of his services, just in case he would be needed, and with a young family, this was usually the case. So Dr Wenjon was never going to be rich, but he was affluent enough, even before the war, to afford a motor car, which in those days was extremely rare. Bessie well remembered the days when, along with the doctor's own family, they all sat in the car as he visited his housebound patients in this close-knit practice. In fact, she spent so much time in the company of the Wenjon family that many thought she was one of them. Her mother never worried about Bessie, as she always knew exactly where she was, along at the Wenjons' home, either with his family or running his errands.

Such errands often placed a great responsibility on the shoulders of such a young child and today would be totally inappropriate. It often involved a visit to the local pharmacist, where she would collect packages to be delivered directly to the doctor, the contents of which were unknown to Bessie. Another task was to regularly visit the local butcher, where she would collect the doctor's weekly order of lamb's liver. Dr Wenjon, at his own expense, then distributed portions of this delicacy to those of his patients he thought required a boost in their iron level.

He was a fastidious person and well ahead of his time when the health and well-being of his patients were involved. This was apparent in the most fundamental of details. One afternoon, the doctor decided to buy each child in his house, which included Bessie, a bag of fish and chips (a fish supper). Of course, it was Bessie who was sent, so with money in hand, off she marched to the chip shop (or chipper) to make the purchase, followed by the rest of his children. In those days, chip shops opened in late afternoon, and this was their first sale of the day. On her return, they opened the bags, but before the feast could commence, the doctor interrupted the proceedings. On a rough piece of paper, he quickly wrote that no one should be expected to eat yesterday's chips. The gang of kids then returned to the shop, with Bessie at the head, note in hand. The embarrassed shop owner, who was not all too pleased, made a new batch of fried chips specially for them. As he handed over these extra-large bags, the owner whispered sheepishly, "Next time, tell me it's for Dr Wenjon and I'll fry fresh chips for you."

CHAPTER 8

The Dundee People

The Millworkers

In the early twentieth century, there was no such thing as paid holidays; instead, there were lockouts, when the mills closed for maintenance and general repair of machinery and cleaning of the thick jute dust that had accumulated on and under the looms. Such lockouts occurred during the last week in August and became an ideal time for the owners and their families to holiday abroad.

Some desperate workers were kept on during this period, but most were idle, many of whom looked for work on the land fruit gathering (berry picking). Here, gang masters would organise scores of workers from the city for work on the local farms. Often these workers would live at the farm where they worked, in their own makeshift tents and shacks; there was no running water, no sanitation, and little privacy. The farmers supplied the workers with food, and some of the better ones supplied accommodation, but the conditions were still extremely poor and unhygienic.

Once back at work in the mills, wages were so low that one could not afford to stay off, for any reason. Absentees due to marriage, funerals, and sickness all went without pay. According to some mill masters, those were hardly valid reasons for taking time off work.

On Saturday, the factories closed at noon. Even Christmas Day was a working day, which was the normal practice in Scotland. Neither the church nor the mill masters appeared to recognise that such a day was worthy enough to be a public holiday, at least for the millworkers. Later, a half day off work was afforded at Christmas, and I still remember my mother coming home from work and preparing Christmas dinner for the family, having worked from six o'clock in the morning. New Year's Day was a lockout, like that of the so-called Dundee holiday week.

It was a hard life, especially for the women. If you had a job, then you kept it come what may, and that often meant enduring the factory's first line of authority, which was the foreman or "gaffer." Life was bad enough without incurring his wrath; he could sack you on the spot, often for no apparent reason other than a personal dislike. These people held great power over the rest of their fellow workers, who were often at the mercy of a foreman's unreasonable demands. They were only millworkers like the rest but had been elevated by the management for their loyalty and tough attitude towards their fellow workers. Most foremen were reasonable people, but many were not, and often workers suffered at the hands of these grandiose upstarts.

Against this background, my grandfather (Steven Keenen McElroy) stood out as a genteel man. I always believed that if circumstances were different, then he would have been a professional person; he had so much to offer and contribute. Instead, he worked long, hard hours or endured endless days of idleness with no income, but he did his best for the family, without much pleasure in return. However, Steve had his own way of escaping the harshness of life's realities. He was well read, and although he played no musical instrument, he had an appreciation of good music. There had been talent in the family. His father played the cornet and his brother the violin. Steve had been an altar boy in St Mary's Chapel and appreciated music from an early age. Bessie often accompanied her father during the warm Sunday afternoons to the local Dudhope park. There, a brass band was always playing, and he would describe and explain the different types of music they were listening to. This was so vivid in my mother's memory, sitting side by side in the sunshine with her dad, just listening until it was time to head home for tea.

Steve was a carpetmaker and spent most of his working life in Gilroy's jute factory in North Tay Street. He was exceptionally proud of his work as it was considered an exacting luxury trade in the jute industry. Bessie, as a young schoolgirl, loved visiting her father while he was at work, a privilege granted only to a few. She would watch in amazement the exquisite, coloured yarn coming together to produce high-quality jute-backed carpets that were renowned abroad and exported all over the world. In turn, this brought fame and wealth to the city, but unfortunately, this wealth did not find its way down to the lowly jute workers on the shop floor. They remained poor and deprived of the dignity that they merited; for a meagre 10/9p (just over fifty pence), these people had to work six twelve-hour shifts per week. At that time in the suburb of Broughty Ferry, there were more millionaire tycoons in one square mile than anywhere else in the world, all begotten from "King Jute."

Baxter, Grant, Grimond, Walker, Caird, Cox, Gilroy, and many more jute barons have all gone, along with the dust, smell, and noise of their jute mills. Only a few memories remain of this recent past, including several chimneys and jute factories that have been either left derelict or recycled for an array of purposes. Reminiscences are all that are left. Thank goodness.

Many of the mills are still standing, including the old mill in which my grandfather spent most of his working life, Gilroy. It now accommodates a sport centre and halls of residence for students of both Dundee and Abertay universities. This is a sign of Dundee once again reinventing itself, still remembering its past by recycling from bygone days, thus retaining part of its history. In this way, Dundee citizens remember the past, to which there is no intent to return. Still standing on Constitution Road (or Brae) is the Gilroy Mansion, which at one time overlooked the old Meadow Bleaching Greens, where my mother and grandmother spent many long, backbreaking hours washing for the family. Farther down this steep brae was once the New Howff Cemetery, which unfortunately was officially dishonoured by decree of the 1960s city council. It was replaced by a little used, concrete, multi-storey carpark. To this day, to me, the reasoning behind such a provocative move is puzzling. Surely it was not simply for profit.

Dancing in the Mill

In time, Bessie came to terms with her lost ambition and settled into her role as a working Dundee lass. As the years went on, her brother Jim finished his apprenticeship and started work as a journeyman painter with a small local firm. Bessie no longer needed to hand over her wage to help keep the family; now she was independent and on full board. She had always been fond of dancing, and as she grew into her teen years, this started to occupy an ever-increasing part of her social life. Bessie felt that she could have danced morning, noon, and night—and very often did. Perhaps it was her way of releasing pent-up, frustrated energy at the loss of her dreams.

Most of her friends were also dancing fanatics. Even during their working day, they would dance—whenever the chance arose. They would dance along the aisles between the jute frames, in their bare feet. This was usually during a tea break or lunch hour, when they ran out of work, or when the loom was broken, which not surprisingly happened quite often. They would dance the set pieces of the Scottish country dances, with one half of the girls taking the place of the men, swinging each other almost off their feet while they clapped and hooched to the "Virginia and Eightsome Reels," "the Dashing White Sergeant," and "Strip the Willow." They never seemed to tire, and when the machinery restarted, they would continue their working shift as usual.

It was during such a dancing fling that Bessie's long hair, which was normally tied back, became caught in the yarn of one of the adjacent machines that were still working. She remembered pulling back hard as the machinery pulled her in. Bessie pulled so hard that some of her hair was ripped from the back of her head—and she could do nothing but scream. A quick-thinking friend just managed to switch the jute frame off in the nick of time. Some men then ran over to help. They held her in position while they cut the entwined yarn and to her great relief finally freed her. Bessie was eternally grateful to her hero friend, who had the presence of mind to stop the machinery; otherwise, there would have been a disfiguring accident, or worse. Nevertheless, Bessie had had an extremely bad shock, and had to suffer, once again, a bald patch that lasted for months. An extreme telling-off from the gaffer then followed, and all the girls were instructed to check that their hair was tight and securely tied back while at work. Dancing in the aisles was also banned, for a few weeks, but it quickly resumed as the management regarded it as a morale booster. Although she was lucky to have come off so lightly, dancing was still in Bessie's blood, so she quickly resumed her place in the aisles along with the rest of the girls, but with her hair well tied back.

When looking back into one's past, there is a tendency to remember mostly the good times and neglect the bad, but as far as the mills were concerned, it was not all dancing in the aisles; it was hard work with long hours and little pay. There was no, or little, compensation for accidents or disfigurement, which often included the loss of a finger (or two) into the machinery, whereby the adjacent worker would take over the operation of the injured party's frame, often without even switching it off. Overhead belts precariously drove the drive shafts of the looms and were operated without hazard guards or warning signs throughout the factory. If a belt snapped or became insecure, it would lash out dangerously in all directions, causing damage and injury to anyone or thing in its way. The occasional lost eye was an injury normally associated with a snapped belt.

They kept the looms running at a rhythmic pace and output, which would be gradually increased as the day went on. Thus, by stealth, they increased the worker's productivity. This was also when the overhead belts were at their most susceptible. To the workers, it was obvious from the higher-pitch tone from these belts that the running speed of the mill had surged. The bosses (management) denied any such increase. From one flat to next, the word would quickly spread, "The mills runnin' fest."

Fire

It was also during this period in the day that the machinery was most likely to catch fire, although fire could spontaneously occur at any time almost anywhere in the mill. This was an obvious daily hazard that the jute worker lived with. Here, any worker who helped control and extinguish an outbreak, which could easily turn into a potentially lethal and explosive situation, was given a bonus payment of threepence. Hence, there was a great rush for the buckets of water and sand that were strategically placed around the mill. The trick in tackling a jute fire was not to throw all the water onto the blaze at once; instead, small amounts should be directly applied to quench the flames. In this way, the fire could be isolated, controlled, and put out.

The first of many such fires of Bessie's forty years in the Dundee mills was the most memorable for her and her gaffer. At the sudden outburst of the fire, she was told to run, get a bucket of water, and throw it on the flames. This she did with great haste and excitement. Unfortunately, her watery contribution passed more through the flames than on them; in fact, through and all over the gaffer who was dousing them from the other side. Fortunately for Bessie, the gaffer was a good-natured man, but at that instant in time, he was not a happy one. Once the fire was out, he called her over. "Bessie," he said, looking straight at her with the sternest of stares, "Ye drooket me, ye daft gouck."[16] His eye then softened ever so slightly but just as quickly narrowed once again to a hard glower. "What are yi?" he asked. With her head hung low, she replied, "Am a daft gouck." He turned, and as he walked away, he flippantly pointed and sent her back to her frame. The telling-off was over, but she could hear him muttering above the squelching of his soaked shoes, "Daft

---

[16] "You have soaked me, you daft thing."

wuman." Bessie also turned and walked away, and with her back to the foreman, a big beaming smile spread over her face as she strode over to her friends. They had witnessed the whole scenario, from the start of the fire, which by then didn't even feature, as they joked and laughed about a soaked gaffer, which was by far funnier than a mere inferno.

However, a jute fire was an extremely dangerous situation for anyone to find themselves in, but the safety of the workers was apparently secondary to that of production and profit; it was understood that the workers would stay and fight any fire. After all, their livelihood depended on it. Hence, the machines had to be up and running as soon as possible. The jute workers (who were on piece work rates)[17] accepted these everyday hazards as part of the norm. The jute unions were not strong enough to do anything that was effective. It had always been that way. Jute fires could spring up almost anywhere in the mills or warehouses, even the harbour dockland where the bails were stored in enormous sheds ready for distribution throughout the city. A potential fire could smoulder for days, especially in damp conditions, before erupting into a ball of flame due to exploding jute bails, which then showered the adjacent areas with burning strands of raw fibre. It was even worse in the mills, where the jute was refined and spun into yarn, which ran through the winding looms onto bobbins or larger spools, which in turn caused combustible dust particles to thicken the air. Fires were often caused by the friction between machine parts and the yarn moving rapidly over them. When combustion did happen, a burst of flame would run along the entire length of the frame, following the path of the yarn through the machinery. Dust on and below the machine would burst into a wall of fire, and even fibres in the air would ignite, often causing a worker to be momentarily engulfed in the inferno. In such a firestorm, rarely was their serious injury as the airborne fibres burnt out quickly; nevertheless, it did leave behind a rather shocked and disorientated machine operator whose eyebrows,

---

[17] Pay per unit production.

eyelashes, and arm and hand hair were badly singed. Normally, due to the immediate response of the employees who were well versed and unafraid of such situations, the fire would be contained within the one flat or level of the mill, often confined to a single machine.

Once the excitement had died down and the fire was out, the foreman often allowed a short tea break while the machinery was checked over, during which the chat would be about who the hero was this time; after that, the flat would then resume work as normal. On rare occasions when a fire raged out of control, a major incident would be declared whereby part, if not all, of the mill would be evacuated; the local firefighting service would then be called in to take over. The mill owners were well insured for such eventualities, but of course it was bad news for the workers. They had no such insurance or compensation, just a lost job and no wage.

The Old Dundee Centre

The jute mills were large, monolithic buildings, and with their tall chimney stacks, they dominated the city's landscape. In fact, each Sunday evening, from the village of Newport on the opposite side of the River Tay, Dundee could not be seen for the thick, bellowing smoke that belched from these great vertical peaks. This was referred to as smoking-up when the mill boilers were fired up in preparation for the following week's work.

Despite the numerous mills in the city, the centre of Dundee was free of these massive dull constructions. Instead, there was a hotchpotch assortment of old streets and houses occasionally intermingled with open spaces and beautiful buildings. These buildings included the city churches, the Old Steeple, and the Town House, which was a rectangular building fronted by seven Roman arches, which were supported by pillars, the whole building was collectively known as the *Pillars*. Nevertheless, during working days, the entire city was normally hazed in a blanket of light smog. The Old Town House stood on the south side of the High Street and was the ideal place for young couples to meet as it was central and provided shelter and a certain amount of privacy. Behind this, to the south of the High Street, was a lane that led to the Vaults, which was a wine merchant's establishment.

At the edge of the dockland area stood the Royal Victoria Arch, and in front of this was the popular Green Market. It was to this open-air market that my grandparents took their young family each Saturday morning. Here, Dundonians could shop cheaply and be entertained. Swings, hobbyhorses, and all sorts of open-air stalls made it a favourite with children, so it was a popular and busy place. Bessie and her young brother, Jim, thought that everything one could think of was sold here. Also, among the crowds of people were the usual notable worthies, including blind Jock, who would read from a Braille Bible, a penny was always dropped into his tin. Farther along, they would find a blind woman playing a melodion and singing what Bessie thought were rude songs. Deeper into the crowded market, always the same two men could be found, one playing the fiddle and the other the bone crackers. Often farmworkers from outside the city would accompany this musical duet by dancing to their tunes, which of course, would encourage others to follow suit. Other features included the bearded lady, the lion-faced man, and the wild man from the jungle, Ooshie Wah. Medicines that would cure almost anything could be bought, and it was possible to have an aching tooth pulled by a giant of a black man using only his fingers. He didn't even bother to wash his hands between patients; he just wiped the blood off.

Before leaving for home, the family would descend upon the buster stall, which was the treat of the day. They all sat down on hard, wooden benches contained in a large homemade tent, the length of a house and half as wide. It was lit only by paraffin flares, and everything was cooked in a massive, black, iron pot heated on a coke fire. It is difficult to describe the culinary delight in tasting a buster. It can only be fully appreciated by eating one in the environment in which it was meant to be eaten. It consisted of a plate of the most delicious chips surrounded by hot, mushy peas; vinegar and salt were then added to taste. I have always enjoyed a buster and can therefore appreciate the taste and smell that they experienced – "Mmm, delicious". Nevertheless, such unhygienic conditions would not be tolerated today. In fact, health and safety representatives would have something to say about the Green Market as a whole. However, it was the best way to eat a buster. In the height of the summer, the market staged an additional attraction, Lady Mary's Fair (St Mary being the patron saint of the city). This fair attracted people from all over the surrounding districts. Everything was at bargain price, including tea sets, linen, jewellery, and all that was needed for a wedding couple's bottom drawer.

The whole of the market was dominated by the Royal Victoria Arch, which acted as a showpiece entrance to the city. Made from local sandstone, it had three large Roman arches supporting four chimney-like structures on top. This was an extremely impressive monument and symbolic of Dundee's tall, smoky stacks. It was a solid piece of Victorian architecture, built in 1853 to celebrate the queen's visit to the city along with Prince Albert, in 1844. It was unique, and the citizens of the city were extremely proud of their arch. However, in time, the city fathers became less enamoured by this icon of the city; they did not fully appreciate the artistic value of such an appealing structure and allowed it to fall into disrepair and neglect. As it declined, and predictably, once again, the city fathers dishonoured themselves and the city by displaying the extent of their limited aesthetic imagination by knocking it down. The confines of their narcissistic arrogance did not stop there, as they then dumped the remains of Dundee's Royal Victoria Arch into the adjacent watery dock, like a discarded pile of garbage. Insult was then added to injury as any remaining evidence of that beautiful monument was without ceremony cast into a local rubbish pit, "the Coup." This shameful and deliberate act of official vandalism has resonated down through the decades. It was indeed ineradicable loss to the city and its citizens.

It was not beyond the bounds of the city's talented tradesmen to have periodically cleaned its tarnished brickwork and left it where it was, which would be now on the north edge of the Slessor Gardens along the waterfront. Or, in a less vehement way, disassembled the arch and reassembled it elsewhere. After all, the Wishart Arch (East Port Gate), in a similar way, was transferred to its present location. An ideal site for the relocation of the arch would have been at the entrance to Camperdown Park, which is a vast public parkland on the outskirts of the city. This estate, now the property of the citizens of Dundee, had once been gifted to Admiral Camperdown for his naval victory over the Dutch. Hence, with such history it would have been a fitting and appropriate new home for the arch. However, it is now something that present and future generations of the city can only appreciate through photographs, paintings, and slowly dying memories; its loss is a stain that may not be forgotten or forgiven.

The Newtyle Rail Line

In addition to the buildings and arches in the centre of Victorian Dundee, it was also an important busy rail junction connected to Perth to the west and the coastal regions of the country to the east.

To the north-west side of the city centre lay the main industrialised heart of the Dundee burgh. Just to the north of the Old Howff Cemetery, the Dundee-Newtyle rail junction was completed and opened in 1831. From here, at present-day Parker Street, a funicular rail line hauled the Newtyle bound carriages up the steep ascent of the Dundee Law (a one in ten gradient) and through the Law Tunnel. There are still remnants of the terminal's infrastructure in Parker Street itself, along with the old staircase that runs up to Barrack Road. It was from here that the funicular would have ascended to the Law Tunnel. The line then followed a hazardous journey out to Newtyle, which at that time was an uninhabited terminal.

By 1837, the rail line had been extended to the city's harbour, thus allowing jute cargo to be transferred to local villages in the Strathmore Valley. Here, with a good supply of fast-flowing water, these rural villages had long been involved in the cotton, and later jute, industry, and it was hoped that the enhanced communication of a rail link would benefit the whole of the County of Angus, along with agricultural expansion. This was not to be, and the opening of the lines from the Newtyle terminal out to the villages of Coupar Angus and Glamis, both in 1837, proved to be unsuccessful.

Closer to the Dundee Burgh, part of this Newtyle rail line swung west to include the suburb of Lochee. Part of this line then branched off to include the private terminal of Cox's Camperdown Jute and Hemp Works. These branches, along with the whole of the Newtyle, line are now obsolete and finally closed in 1955. However, the Law Tunnel is still there, but the entrance and exit are now blocked, and the tunnel is closed to the public. Perhaps this could be yet another additional and exciting development for the City of Discovery.

Dundee's Royal Half Mile

The most common form of socialising was by far to be found in many of the pubs located throughout Dundee. Drunkenness was a problem in these days, perhaps due to the high unemployment level among the menfolk. Dundee was a city for women workers. This was due to their nimble fingers in operating the jute looms and their ability to swiftly repair broken yarn as it wound its way through the noisy machinery, by quick use of the weaver's knot. The men were often relegated to the home and as a result were nicknamed "kettle boilers[18]." For some weaker men, drink was an easy alternative, which of course made their existing condition even worse. For them, the pub became not an end of day social outlet but an unnecessary infliction on the family, something the wife could well do without. I was lucky as a drink problem for my parents and grandparents was never an issue. My folks would often go without to give to my brother, Bill, and then, ten years later, me.

There were few outlets to this deprived situation, but one such oasis where the young could meet and socialise was in the centre of the city. This was the Overgate. Once known as Argyllgait, this

---

[18]   A "kettle boiler" was an unemployed Dundee man.

half-mile-long, narrow street was the hub of Dundee's social life. Even in my parents' youth, the Overgate was centuries old; it even boasted a castle house and turret at its east end. Here, Cromwell's General Monck had set up his headquarters, in 1651, during his siege of the city and assault on the St Marys Tower (the Old Steeple). Regardless of such fascinating history, once again, the city fathers imposed their bulldozing mentality by deciding, this time, to knock the streets of the Overgate down completely. Of course, they would not, could not, demolish the city churches and steeple. The Overgate was replaced by the most hideous of concrete shopping centres imaginable, which only a few decades later was itself demolished. With a little prudence, one would think that at least some elected councillors, somewhere, would have seen the potential and, like the Shambles in York, would have renovated at least part of the old Overgate. With the city's latest venture into the tourist trade, and its desire to attract visitors, chances were missed. So, let's have a little foresight by not allowing such stupid folly to happen again.

Despite its age and deteriorating condition, the Overgate was one of the most popular venues in the city. The Green Market eventually closed and was transferred to the western end of this half-mile-long street. Almost every afternoon, throngs of people would stroll along its length then back, even more so on Saturday. Here, during the evening weekends, dozens of youngsters (teenagers), including me, would wander up and down this narrow street, the boys eyeing up the girls and hopefully vice versa. Youngsters and adults alike enjoyed a visit to Franchise café, an essential ritual, then into the Green Dykes chemist for a sarsaparilla, and if the money stretched that far, over to the market stalls for a buster. It seemed that this was the way it had always been, almost a way of life, and when the Overgate was finally demolished, affairs went out of sorts.

Many of the old landmarks of Dundee have now gone, but their memory stayed particularly with my mother, as if it were only yesterday; the noise, the different smells, and the hustle and the bustle all remained special to her.

But above all, she remembered the friendliness of the people—her people.

A Brief Encounter

My mother, Bessie, met (for the second time) her future husband, Sandy, at the Foresters dance hall. He was a good dancer, and of course, this was to his advantage, so together they danced the night away. She was barely 15, and he was four years older, but that was trivial as they both loved dancing. They met a few times after that, going to the silent movies or, like most young couples, for a walk along the Esplanade waterfront on a Sunday afternoon.

My Father, at the age of 16.

Soon after this, Sandy was called up to serve both king and country in the armed forces, hence the relationship was severed at least for the time being, as was the case for so many young couples.

He was placed with a west coast regiment, the Highland Fusiliers, and shipped straight off to France, apparently before even the start of his basic training.

This was strange to say the least, but it transpired that Sandy had left home when only 16, probably to get as far away from his domineering father as possible, and, lying about his age, joined the Highland Fusiliers. He had completed his basic training before being found by his parents and brought back home, with a little help from his policeman father. With the introduction of conscription, he was then called up and hastily bundled into the fusiliers. He was billeted in Ayrshire along with the rest of his company—all young men, mostly from the Glasgow area, who quickly blended into a tight family. All except one. This was Rab (Robert), a Glaswegian who could only be described as a lowlife reprobate. This man would lie, cheat, and steal from his fellow squaddies. Nothing was safe. Money, property, and even letters went missing. They all knew who was responsible but could prove nothing. In addition to apparently having no family, he made no friends in the billet, despite his efforts to befriend almost everyone with his apparent unrealistic claims and garbled nonsense.

After a few weeks, my father noticed that some recent letters had gone missing. He suspected Rab but could prove nothing, so he had to let it go. However, Sandy's next letter from home caused him to almost explode with temper. Rab had stollen the letters and while on leave had gone to Dundee, to my father's parents, and posed as Sandy's best friend. He was welcomed into the family circle and given the best of their hospitality. In fact, he stayed for a few days before being seen off with food and money. Sandy confronted him with this letter, which Rab had hoped to intercept before my father received it; letters were usually thrown onto the appropriate beds while the whole billet was at breakfast. On that day, Sandy was delayed in the billet and received the letter directly from his sergeant. A fight broke out in the mess hall, and both men were placed on a charge. However, when the facts behind the assault were realised, Sandy's charge was dismissed. But Rab's charge stood. He was placed in detention for one week, and his pay was docked by the amount Sandy's parents had spent on this man. On his release, he appeared to have no remorse over his actions, being more annoyed at being caught. He was subsequently sent to Coventry by the men and was warned by my father to be less worried about the German bullets. Shortly after this incident, the fusiliers were sent off to France, and inevitably the day came that they had all been trained for.

Private Sandy (back row, second left) with the Highland Fusiliers.

A German Soldier

It was a cold day in early December 1918, and the British artillery had been pounding the German lines for an hour with little response from the enemy guns. The men were lined along the frontline trench, some sitting, some squatting, all knowing what lay ahead of them. No fear showed on the faces of those young men, probably for the benefit of others. Ladders were placed at short regular intervals along the full length of the trench, which disappeared on both sides into the morning haze. They all stood to attention as the grim-faced officer in charge appeared. He immediately climbed the ladder, giving the impression that this was a normal, everyday event for him. As he climbed, his whistle shrieked down through the trenches, drowning all else out.

Once directly at the top, he half turned and waved his hand to beckon the rest of his company up and out. "Come on, fusiliers! This is what you're here for!"

At this command, everyone to a man moved forward and prudently climbed the ladders and over the top. If any time mattered in the lives of those frightened young men, it was now. The company sergeant was by now out of the trench and pushing his men forward. "Keep moving, lads, and keep your head down! Remember your training!" he was shouting—something he himself should have remembered. British artillery had become extremely accurate, and the gunners were able to put down a line of fire precisely in front of their own advancing lines. At the start of the war, this accuracy was not the case, and such a bombardment often accounted for 10 per cent of all British casualties (collateral damage). My father was in the second line to move out, and as he stepped into no man's land, his stride lengthened and his pace quickened, as did the rest of his company's. He started to feel a certain amount of elation as his heart reached fever pitch, but this was quickly crushed.

By this time, the full ensemble of enemy artillery and machine-gun fire had started to retaliate. Shells were exploding over the entire battlefield, and there appeared to be total confusion. His sergeant, who was slightly to the front right of my father, was suddenly hit by a piece of spiralling shrapnel from an overhead shell burst. It cut clean through the sergeant's neck, and his entire head parted from his body. His head flew back, hitting the ground with a sickening thump just inches from my father. The rest of the sergeant's lifeless body seemed to continue running forward for a few paces until it collapsed into a motionless heap of dead flesh. It then sank into the mud of no man's land on this World War I battlefield.

Although shocked at the sudden death of his sergeant, Sandy continued forward until he literally fell into the evacuated trenches of the Germans' frontline. However, he was not alone, quickly becoming aware of the presence of another two. They were Germans. One was dead, and the other was wounded but conscious. He posed no threat, and as the medics would be along soon, my father sat beside his enemy. He offered him a cigarette, which he refused, but he readily accepted some water.

As these two men sat side by side in the German trenches, another fusilier stumbled in. It was Rab. My father's hackles rose, his eyes narrowed, and his mouth tightened as he remembered the warning he had given. This was the one man that he literally hated. Sandy slowly rose and moved farther up the trench away from this intruder. It was then that he heard the familiar cocking of a revolver. Thinking that it was Rab about to pre-empt my father's threat, in an instant he swung round. But the threat was not from Rab, instead it came from the wounded German, who was pointing the barrel straight at Sandy's fervent enemy, presumably with the intent to kill one more British soldier. At once and without thinking, Sandy lunged forward, and before the weakening finger of the German could squeeze the trigger and fire, a fixed bayonet stabbed into the German's neck, immediately killing him.

At that, the trench started to fill with fusiliers and the incident passed. Sandy was a Lewis gunner trained to fire at enemy positions, not knowing whether he had killed or injured anyone. But this was different. He had met this man and looked into his face. He had even tried to help him, before launching his bayonet into his neck. If this action had gone farther up the line of command, my father may have received a citation in dispatches or even a medal for saving the life of a fellow soldier. What sort of conventional ideology is this whereby one man is expected to brutally kill another and be rewarded for it?

The fusiliers had done their job, and next morning, they returned to their own lines, being replaced with fresh troops. Eventually, by 1918 they had entered Germany, and Sandy saw first-hand the deprivation and suffering that the German people were enduring, especially the women and children, who were the real victims. These people were the same as us, ordinary working folk. They didn't start the war, but like us, they had to fight it. We had all been hoodwinked into hate and annihilation, Christian nations at each other's throat—all for the self-indulgent greed of a few.

Just after Christmas of that year, he returned to the fusiliers' barracks in Scotland, being demobbed the following spring back into civilian life (civvy street). However, this experience was never forgotten by my father, and it remained a dark cloud that hung over him for the rest of his life. He never attended victory celebrations or remembrance services, and he never saw the point in revelling over a totally unnecessary conflict that, of course, led directly to the Second World War.

Time to Remember (or forget)

On the summit of the Law stands a monument commemorating those who fell during the first and second world wars. This large granite monument, a gift of commemoration from the citizens of Dundee, was unveiled in its present position in 1925, almost one hundred years ago. It is a stark reminder of past carnage and death, and as one visitor to Dundee expressed to me, "It's like a tombstone sitting over the city." I have no doubt there would be many objections if it were to be relocated to a more suitable place. The main protest would be that it has always been there since its construction; it is a daily reminder of those who fell during these dark times in our history. But these were periods that we should be prepared to put behind us and forget forever. There should not be, in this twenty-first century, a continual graphic reminder of the mad endeavours and bloodletting follies of our past leaders, of which this monument is now a reminder, stretching back over the previous one hundred years.

This impressive monument could conceivably be transferred to a more appropriate place in the city. Perhaps the quiet surrounds of Camperdown Park, where those to whom it holds profound meaning can contemplate the aura of its presence in more accessible and intimate surroundings. There, it could be relocated and serenely sit in a well-kept, tranquil garden and not as Dundee's headstone.

Respect and honour must be given to those who gave their lives for our freedom. But now possibly is the time to look forward and strive for the brighter future that they died for and not back at the gruesome gore of the two most catastrophic wars in humankind's history.

That is what the twentieth century will forever be remembered for—when Christian countries slaughtered Christian countries to oblivion, resulting in over 100 million dead[19] and even more lamed, homeless, starved, or diseased. That is nothing to be proud of—nothing to celebrate. My father often said that if a nation deliberately arms itself to the teeth, then it will fight, and that our country could do more with its money than prepare for war.

I think that those who had fought and died in such conflicts would now like us to forget and instead strive for a better future that they had helped provide.

Boston

Once back from the army, Sandy completed his apprenticeship. But this young journeyman now found that there was no work available in the city. He also wanted to see more of the world than just the French trenches and the local shipyard, where he had started work at the age of 13, he gave serious consideration to try his luck in the United States of America. Prior to the war, Sandy had made plans to emigrate to what he thought would be a better life. He did ask my mother if she wanted to leave with him, but that was just juvenile talk; Bessie was far too young to consider any such move. Her father had been idle for some time, and her loyalties were still to her parents and the family. However, although their relationship was still in its infancy, they promised to write and keep in touch. They then parted, perhaps forever.

Sandy left for America at the age of 20, landing in Boston along with the eldest of his brothers, William, who was already married with

---

[19]   20 million in the First World War and 80 million in the Second.

a family that was to follow later. On his arrival in Boston, William found work almost immediately, which was not surprising as he was a member of the Order of Freemasons, an important and influential group in the States. It was some two years later, on his return home, that Sandy was accepted into the Order. In the meantime, he was stuck in a strange land, out of luck, and out of work. The Great Depression had started to take hold over the whole of America, quickly spreading throughout the rest of the world.

This was not a good time to have emigrated to the States, especially to a city like Boston, but my father was there and had to make the best of things. Often when describing Boston, he would repeat the story of his encounter with a local beat policeman. Once while walking home, after a normal unsuccessful day looking for work, he walked through a rundown, poorly lit part of the city. At the end of a long, narrow street, he was met by a large, stocky policeman, truncheon in hand and revolver at the ready. "And where have you come from?" he asked in a clear, unforgettable Irish accent. My father was tired and didn't have time for chit-chat with a policeman; he had had enough of that back home. "I've been looking for work up there," my father quickly quipped back. The policeman grinned and with a surprising look said, "You're a Scot, from Dundee I reckon? I've been there. I recognise your twang." It transpired that he had emigrated from Cork in Ireland to the jute city before trying his luck in America. These two men immediately established an invisible Celtic bond. My father was told that he was lucky to be alive, as the street he had just walked along was the most dangerous in the city. Even the police did not venture down this notorious gang-ruled thoroughfare; it was a "no go area." Sandy was then given some good advice on how to live in an American city like Boston during these depressed years. The advice boiled down to this: "Trust no one as everybody has an angle, and finally, everything in America will in some way cost you."

My father did not fully accept this advice. Perhaps it had been given in good faith, but it was given through prejudicial eyes of a fellow immigrant. There was much good in the American character, which Sandy had experienced. However, he was never overwhelmed by the country as a whole and understood only too well what this Boston policeman was trying to say. Despite the depression, the country was young and developing fast, and its people had become too brash, at least for my father's eyes. And although he was by no means a soft man, he preferred the more easy-going nature of his fellow Dundonians.

Nevertheless, he persevered in this land of opportunity, taking work wherever he could find it—bars, docks, building sites, or anywhere—to no avail. Then, while in Boston, he was once again stricken by his old nemesis. He contracted a form of dermatitis, which had dogged my father all his working life. It would start on one of his fingers and spread to his hands and then to the lower part of his arms. While in Boston, he consulted doctors and attended hospitals, often costing him a week's wage and more, until during one hospital visit, he met a doctor who happened to be a fellow Scot. His advice was not what my father expected. He was told that if he wanted the infection to clear, then go home. In the States, they were simply supplying ointment that would treat the symptoms, but not the cause of the infection. That cost more, which my father could not afford. So after only two years in America, he prepared to return home.

With no money for the fare, he worked his passage across the ocean on a cattle boat bound for Liverpool. During this voyage, he helped to successfully deliver a calf; this was no problem for my father, as he had spent much of his youth working on a farm. This was the Hillocks farm just on the outskirts of Burrelton, a small village fifteen miles north of Dundee. With such a skill at his fingertips, Sandy was offered a full-time job on board, travelling back and forth across the Atlantic, but he was set on returning home. After all, he had to meet my mother again.

Sandy outside the huts for immigrants, outskirts of Boston.

While in America, Sandy and his brother Will had clearly gone their own separate ways. Sandy was single with no commitments, but his brother's intention was to bring his family out to Boston, which he eventually did. Will's family consisted of his wife (Judith), his daughter (Edith), and his son (Ronald); both siblings were in their teenage years when they left Dundee and were only slightly younger than their uncle Sandy. They had all found a job, so Will's plan to resettle was working, at least for the time being. Unfortunately, this did not last, probably due to the unfavourable times and the hardships that were starting to be felt at every level of society. William decided that the best plan would be to return to Scotland. This was not an easy decision and was not to the liking of his wife or grownup family, who had all adapted better than their father to this new life. He saw no prospects for himself, and this placed great pressure on the marriage, which after a few years fell apart. The couple, who had started anew with so much hope, divorced. Soon after this, William departed his adopted country and returned home—alone.

None of Will's family returned to their hometown until both parents had died and they themselves had retired. However, they always referred to Dundee as "home," and once retired, they returned to the city of their birth each year until their visits were curtailed due to deteriorating health. Edith and Ronald were my direct cousins, and I met them on each of their annual pilgrimages to the "homeland."

My great-niece, Cathern Pullar, who lived on the outskirts of Dundee, in the village of Carnoustie, provided them with a home base as they toured the places that brought back so many old memories. Cathern, who was headmistress of the Carlogie Primary School in the village, looked forward to their annual visits, which coincided with Cath's long summer holiday. She always accompanied them on their daytrip excursions. Finally, at the end of each holiday, the older members of the family, which included my mother and father, all met to reminisce about their collective past and the bygone years. And they did not forget to visit the family's ancestral home, which was the Hillocks farmhouse, close to Burrelton, by the village of Coupar Angus. In so doing, they would descend annually upon Margaret Findlay, who at that time was the oldest living relative of the extended Pullar family. She eventually lived to the age of 102, having spent her entire life in this part of the country, so she knew the old family well, and its history. Much of this history she related to me, but sadly a considerable amount died with her.

Ill health eventually stopped these pleasantly nostalgic visits of my American cousins. Then one day I received word that both Edith and Ronald had passed away within months of each other, both in their eighties. Edith had a daughter and two sons, but Ronald had no family, which meant that this American part of the family name was discontinued. Not long after this, Cathern, who remained a devoted spinster, died at the young age of 69, from cancer.

CHAPTER 9

Reminiscence

The General Strike of 1926

My father, who had returned home from America after only two years abroad, found that Dundee was by no means immune to the now worldwide depression. This catastrophe caused acute hardship in the city, which experienced its share of riots and discontent.

However, it was my mother, in her early twenties, who clearly remembered the day that she and her friend Meg Morris were on their way to the Cinerama picture house in Tay Street. They were stopped in the town by a few young lads and warned to go no farther as there was a riot going on in the town centre. Neither girl knew what a riot was, and of course they innocently went off to have a look. Things seemed peaceful enough as they walked along the Murraygate. However, as they approached the High Street, they could not believe what they were looking at. People were screaming and running in all directions, and one man was covered in blood from a head wound. The police were out in force and meant serious business. They thrashed into the public, striking them down hard with their long batons.

This was the start of the General Strike, and the strikers had taken exception to anyone else doing their work. A cart fully loaded with jute bails had been untethered and shoved by a few strikers into the docks. Some then attempted to march up Crichton Street. The police had surrounded the council building at the Pillars of the old Townhouse, on the High Street, and as more of them arrived on horseback and in closed vans, they went straight into action against the crowd. For a while, both men and a few brave women stood their ground as the onslaught continued until eventually their lines broke and they scattered. In the panic that followed, Bessie momentarily lost Meg, but she was suddenly ushered into an alleyway where Meg was sheltering. Their rescuer was a friend of Meg, who ironically was an officer of RSPCA (Royal Society for the Prevention of Cruelty to Animals) and lived in a top-storey flat in Crichton Street opposite the Pillars of the Town House.

There, from a window, they had a grandstand view of this unbelievable fiasco that was going on in the streets below. None of them could believe that this was Dundee; law and order had broken down, and it was the police who were running riot. From their vantage point, they witnessed a sailor, with kitbag over his shoulder, attempting to weave his way through the police lines on his way to the rail station. The police were allowing him through, but one brave mounted officer decided to baton him down and with a few hard blows split his head open. As the police lines moved forward, they left him lying in the gutter in his own blood. My mother said that she would never forget what happened next. The sailor rose to his feet and with blood still streaming down his face he held his head up. With a slight stagger at first, he picked up his stride, and with kitbag again slung over his shoulder and a dignified courage, walked towards the second line of advancing police. They were more respectful of this brave, plucky serviceman and their line opened to allow him through—the least they could do.

Eventually, things quietened down in the Crichton Street area and the two girls decided to run for home, which was on the other side of the town centre. They ran back along the Murraygate until they found themselves stopped once again by a second crowd that was forming at the Wellgate Steps. The police were preventing anyone crossing Victoria Road, and for the girls, that meant they could not get home. The people were peaceful, just waiting to disperse back to their homes, when a feeling of unease spread through the assembled mass; this was fanned by a rumour that more police were on their way from Aberdeen. Their unease quickly turned to fear as down Victoria Road drove what seemed like an army of black vans. These were the rumoured reinforcements. The vans screamed to a halt, and as their doors burst open, dozens of fresh police officers spilled out and immediately battered their way into the peaceful crowd, among them Bessie and Meg. For a while, these unarmed men stood. Some shouted that the crowd was peaceful and contained women, others tried to fight back, but all was in vain. For a while, the two girls were in the middle of this bewildering melee. But in just a few seconds, an elderly man saw a chance for the girls to dash across Victoria Road. He did his best to hold back the panicking mayhem of people. "Run! Run!" he shouted at them.

Still frightened and disorientated, they ran as fast as they could across what seemed to be an ever-widening expanse of road to relative safety. Victoria Road had become the dividing line between the warzone arena to the south of the circular steps of the Wellgate and, to the north, the peaceful but terrified spectators who had accumulated at the bottom of the Hilltown Brea. Once across, they followed their own way home; Meg ran up the Hilltown, and Bessie along Dudhope Street turning into Dallfield Walk, sprinting all the way. There, her mother, who had seen the mounted police ride along the side streets, had no idea what had happened to her family and was frantic with worry.

At last, the family started to appear. First was 10-year-old John, who had been playing football and knew nothing of the trouble, followed by Jim, who had been chased by the police but managed to escape unscathed, and finally, Bessie, who was totally exhausted. On seeing her daughter home safely, Mary broke down in tears, one of the few occasions that Bessie had seen her mother show real emotion. It was this display of concern and affection from her mother that most touched Bessie, and they both cried and hugged. They were all safe.

The next night, trouble was still brewing in the city, and the family was banned from going out. Bessie had no intensions of leaving the safety of the house, but her brother had other ideas. He was stopped by his father, who found a "tattie chapper" (potato chopper) hidden up Jim's jumper. He was only 14 years old but had every intension to defend himself and to fight back. This seemed to amuse his sister as she tried to imagine Jim and this small tattie chapper matched against a six-foot-tall policeman with a hard wooden truncheon at his disposal.

During this disordered chaos, Bessie's future father-in-law (Grandfather Pullar) had been watching events unfold from his back-bedroom window, which overlooked the steep slope of the Hilltown. As mounted police rode past and down towards the city centre, this stubborn retired policeman who was half hanging out of the window had to be dragged back by his sons into the room. "Gee it ti them lads,"[20] he was calling, waving his uniformed colleagues on as they passed. Despite the quick response from the whole family, who knew exactly what the police were doing, the old man remained adamant. He then attempted to return to the window to continue his skewed support for the police, and the sons had to forcibly restrain him. Finally, it took his wife's intervention to calm the turmoil. "For god sake man di yi want us a ti be lynched?"[21] Johanne shouted at the obstinate old man. Taking the side of the sons and standing up to her husband was an extremely unusual course of action for this normally quiet woman to take, but it was necessary. At this, he appeared to see sense and calmed down, but he was not a happy man.

---

[20]   "Give it to them, lads."
[21]   "For God's sake man, do you want us all to be lynched?"

Grandfather Pullar (the auld man).

As things got back to normal, the memory of the riots dimmed comparatively quickly into the past. Also, although still in a depressed state, the Dundee people remained good natured and were still readily willing to forgive misdemeanours of the past, but such demeanours were not as easily forgotten, as events were later to prove.

The Fife Miners

However, in many ways, things were even worse for the coal miners of Fife. They were almost starved back to work with little if anything to show for their militant action. Their conditions of work were as bad and, in some cases, worse than those in the jute mills. The coal-face miners were often expected to crawl into and dig out, by pick and shovel, seams of coal often only eighteen inches thick. This often resulted in tragic and frequent roof collapses with the inevitable loss of life. If a coal seam roof did collapse, it would often result in the release of poisonous coal gas or flooding of the mine. Miners would often be trapped underground for days, even weeks, as their colleagues on the surface frantically tried to dig them out as anxious loved ones nervously looked on.

Like the millworkers of Dundee, there was little compensation or sympathy for the bereaved widows and families. Charity funds were set up for such families, but they came nowhere near meeting the grieving needs of a wife or mother. During the strike, groups of undernourished miners often came to Dundee in a plea for food and if possible, money. The strikers of the city, who were themselves in dire straits, did their best to help alleviate the hardship of these stricken miners and their families. Food, clothes, and where possible, money were passed to these fellow suffering workers from Fife. Without assistance from state or church, some working-class Dundee families temporarily accepted into their own homes the neediest of the miners' children until the worst of the crisis was over, when they were then reunited. This was something that the mining community of Fife never forgot about the Dundee people. There was a close bond between the two communities until the Seafield pit closed in 1988, followed by more deprivation for Fife.

As a child, I remember this bond in the late 1940s. During the last week of July and the first week of August, all Dundee mills and factories closed; this was the city's now holiday fortnight. During the first week of this fortnight, my parents always booked a short holiday in the Fife village of Buckhaven, on the Firth of Forth. They did this each year as they found the mining community friendly and warm, a bit like themselves. However, my father once recalled having arranged lodgings with a mining family, who had a room to rent for that week. Off we all went, looking forward to a whole week away from the smoke of the city. Once there, my father had to find the house, and like any man, he walked into the local pub to inquire. There, the barman and locals remembered him from previous years, and he was immediately made to feel welcome, but there was a sudden distinct coolness in their attitude when he asked about the person and address that he was looking for. A bit miffed, my father left the pub; this was not like the miners he knew.

As he walked away, one of the pub locals caught up with him and explained this odd behaviour. The man my father was looking for had been a strike-breaker during the General Strike and was regarded as a black leg (or scab). This was an extremely derogatory term, and this strike-breaker had been ostracised by his fellow workers. This was more than twenty years after the strike, but still no one claimed to know him. However, seeing that my folks were in a quandary, this local directed us to the address. Once there, we were all made welcome, but there was not the expected banter that was normal from a mining family. They appeared to have friends, but only within a small exclusive circle—probably other strike-breakers. From my memories, I enjoyed myself, but my parents were uneasy; my father was a strong trade unionist and would never have walked through or crossed a picket line. We never returned to that address.

The General Strike started at midnight on 4 May 1926 and lasted nine days. It was due to the harsh, austere measures imposed upon the working-class people by a coalition government formed between the Liberal and Conservative political parties. Starting with a general strike of miners, who were expected to increase their working hours for less pay, it resulted in a lockout of strikers across the entire country. As the pits were made idle, sympathy strikes spread throughout the land, which caused great hardship to already ailing families. Although the miners stayed out until November, in the end, the strike was called off with no concessions given by the mine owners. In other words, the strike was broken.

In 1927 the Trade Union Dispute Act was passed, which outlawed sympathy striking, only to be overturned by the Labour government in 1946. However, the Thatcher government of 1980 banned secondary sympathy striking. Overall, the government won, but it left a bitter legacy and bad memories between workers and employers. Many firms, such as the publishing firm D C Thomson of Dundee, were non-union establishments, and along with their non-Catholic policy, they only added to the resentment. Things, of course, have now changed.

Despite the Depression

Despite still being in the shadow the Great Depression with its continued unrest, poor living conditions, and relentless idleness, which was always part of Dundee's speckled history, the Dundee psyche, strange as it may seem, still had energy enough for fun and enjoyment. Bessie would often dash home from a hard day in the mill, help her mother with the cleaning and meals, and then start preparing for a night out—of course, dancing.

In such a small house with a large mixed family, bathing and personal privacy were restricted and certainly rationed. A head to foot wash was often done at the kitchen sink, while the rest of the family occupied themselves in the backroom. Jim, who was also a dancer, would brush his shoes and press his one and only suit while waiting on his sister finishing her ablutions. They would then change over with the typical brother and sister exchange of banter as they passed each other. It would then be Bessie's turn to press her clothes and brush her hair. This was the usual Friday night ritual and often during the working week, all to the amusement of the rest of the family. Their father, Steve, just shook his head and continued reading the evening paper; their mother, Mary, would complain about the disruption to her routine. The two siblings would then walk out together, off to meet their respective friends at their own preferred dance hall, still exchanging the same mischievous repartee of sibling taunts. There, they would stay until the end, and then look for another hall where they would continue their dancing till the early hours of the morning, totally unconcerned that Saturday was a working day.

Each end of the town had its own dance halls, and Bessie had visited them all. With only a few hours of sleep, they would again start work and complete a full shift. This was genuine enjoyment, probably due to the drudgery of their everyday working lives. All that was on the minds of these young people was fun. There was no alcohol sold in any dance hall, only soft drinks, but the young men prior to this would normally have gone to the pub. The women would chatter and entertain themselves until just after half past nine, when the pubs closed. The men would then appear, full of nonsense and fun but without the trouble that seems so pronounced among today's youth. Anyone making a nuisance of himself was quickly dealt with by the other men, who overall were polite and respectful to the girls. The girls in return were expected to dance with whosoever asked. These were the rules in all the dance halls, and if there was no good reason, such as drunkenness, a girl could be asked to leave the hall if she refused a young man's request.

This was a generation that learnt all the modern dance steps, which included the foxtrot, waltz, and quickstep, but also the Scottish country dances. The women attended dance classes and were quite proficient at most routines, whereas the men were not and often learnt from their girlfriend or sister, which was the case for Jim, who turned out to be a particularly good dancer. How well a boy could dance was often the main topic under discussion among the young girls; this was of extreme importance. Hence, it was a matter of crucial reputation that a lad should be able to competently take the floor. Each hall throughout the city had its good male dancers, and great prestige was to be had among the lassies if asked to take to the floor by one of them.

During this time, Bessie's best friend was Meg Morris, and they spent many long hours attending such classes, sometimes in the Foresters Hall in Nicoll Street, which originally was home to the Ancient Order of Foresters and later became the Rep Theatre before it was destroyed by fire. But normally these classes were held in the City Assembly Rooms at the end of Dundee's Exchange Street. It was Mr James Duncan and his wife who ran the classes, both of whom often travelled to the larger cities, including London, where they received instructions in the latest steps and modern trends. This was the Duncan's' main venue, and like all city dance halls, the evening would start off with "The Grand March." At some point during the evening's proceedings, the proprietor and his wife would introduce a new set of dance steps. They would then choose different partners to lead off this new dance. To be chosen as a lead-off dancer was regarded as a great honour among these youngsters, and how well he or she performed was often a topic of discussion all evening.

This was during the "dance band" era, and the Duncans decided to open two completely new dance halls in the city, the Palais and Empress. This was a chance to invite many of the currently famous bandleaders and celebrities to the city, which included the most celebrated of all, Victor Sylvester. He personally demonstrated the latest steps to the eager Dundee fans. Once the dance had been demonstrated, he would then lead off by asking one of the ladies to partner him once round the floor before resuming his place as bandleader. My mother's claim to fame was that she once partnered Victor Sylvester in the leadoff for a new dance in the Palais Ballroom in Dundee. Even in her nineties, her mind's eye would step back and recall this claim to fame as she once again stepped back on the dance floor and relived those magical days.

Jim's Booth Boxing Career

As the courtship continued, Bessie recalled the first time her brother, Jim, and Sandy met. It was one Friday evening while the couple were strolling through the carnival (a funfair), which was held annually in Gussie Park, just off Fairbairn Street. Normally, it was a field of mud and cinders where teams of boys would play football after school—and from where John often returned home in a grubby gutter-covered condition. However, all changed when the park hosted the arrival of the carnival. Colourfully lit stalls were set up, including the favourite "roll-a-penny" stalls whereby a single penny, rolled into a square marked with a number on the table, without touching its edges of that square, allowed one to win the same number of pennies as was printed. There were also amusements, swings, and dodgem cars; the idea was not to dodge but to bump the other cars as much as possible.

These were but a few of the attractions and all great fun, but the one feature that Sandy liked most was the booth boxing. Here, the resident booth boxer challenged all comers (in his weight range), and if the challenger survived, which meant still standing at the end of the third round, he would receive his prize money, usually £1, a significant boost to the wage of any millworker. So this attracted much interest from spectators and challengers alike. No premedical check was required, nor was there any need for a doctor to be present during the contests—at least, when the bout started. If the challenger did not last the full three rounds, for any reason, then he got nothing. Well, perhaps a black eye and damaged pride.

In later life, I worked with a one-time booth boxer, and he explained that come what may, they just had to win the fight, whether by legal or foul means. This could mean flicking sand in the eyes of his opponent, low blows, standing on toes, hitting with the inside of the glove, anything to win, and as expected, the resident referee saw nothing. Many amateur boxers tried to earn a little extra by booth boxing, but of course, if this ever came to light, then they would immediately have lost their amateur status, as this was professional prize fighting. Bessie was by no means a lover of blood sports, but she was carried along on Sandy's enthusiasm into the booth boxing tent, where to her surprise there were as many female spectators as there were male, and they were making just as much noise. In the tent's interior, each of the contestants was presented to the audience, and for each challenger, loud choruses of intimidating support reverberated through the tight, confined space. Sandy explained that if the challenger put up a good fight, or if it was entertaining enough, then the spectators could demand that he be paid more than the agreed prize money.

Something memorable always happened during the contest; often the booth boxer's opponent would take cold feet and attempt to escape from the ring, whereupon he would be pushed back in by an extremely vocal and excited crowd. On occasions, one boxer would pursue the other round the ropes for most of the bout; and on occasions, they held on to each other so tightly that they both fell out of the boxing ring altogether. Bessie witnessed most of these strange proceedings, to such an extent that tears of laughter were running down her face. She had never been so entertained in her life. This was real, live comedy. It was even funnier than the music hall turns in the old Vic Theatre. Strangely enough, and to Bessie's surprise, at the end of each bout, both men seemed to be the best of friends and even cuddled each other. Also, nobody appeared to get seriously hurt.

The couple stayed until the last bout, just to see what clownery would finally happen. As the final contestant climbed into the ring, he looked familiar to Bessie. She looked again. "That's Jim!" she cried out. "He's my little brother." Due to the jostling and noise of the crowd, Bessie had neither recognised nor properly heard the initial introductions at the start of the evening. But there was no mistake; it was him. Gloves on and stripped to the waist, he looked every inch a boxer, even waving to the crowd. Bessie hid her face in case he saw her among the spectators, who by this time were cheering him on. Her first thought was what her mother would say, if she ever found out. Her second thought was that he would get hurt, and the third was *How stupid can he get?* She felt like climbing into the ring and dragging him out, but that would have been too humiliating for them both.

"He's up there now," said Sandy. "And we'll just have to wait and see what happens."

Jim had not noticed the couple in the crowd, so he could not blame them for what happened next. Bessie hid behind Sandy but still managed to look over his shoulder towards the ring and her brother. This was the one whom she had always protected and kept safe. What was he thinking about? However, at the back of her mind, she was quite proud. "Jim McElroy is to fight now" was the announcement. Bessie shut her eyes, the bell rang loud and clear, and the fight was on.

Sandy gave her hand a squeeze as the noise rose to fever pitch. Sandy suddenly released her hand as there was an almighty shout from the crowd. Jim was down and wasn't getting up. First punch, first round, and he was out. Bessie asked what had happened. "It's all over" was the reply. "But he's fine and back on his feet."

The crowd immediately started to move towards the tent exits and out. Sandy squeezed through in the opposite direction towards the ring with a relieved Bessie following behind. Jim, still slightly dazed, was sitting in his corner, attempting to pull his shirt back over his sore head. "Well done," said Sandy. "At least you gave it a go."

As Jim looked up at this stranger, he saw his sister standing behind. He could not believe that she was there and saw everything. His first reaction was not to tell their mother. "I won't tell if you don't tell that I was at the booth boxing." Both nodded in agreement and smiled.

The men were introduced to each other, and they shook hands, agreeing that it was just a lucky punch. All three then walked through the carnival together, Jim rather erratically, and then home.

From then on, Jim and Sandy were the best of friends and later brothers-in-law, until Jim died in 1977 at the age of 70.

In the Most Affectionate Way

Bessie's early memories of the family usually only contained Jim, and for a while, they were the only two siblings. Jim was an active child who could be quite studious at times. Like his father, he had an aptitude and an appreciation for music and became quite proficient in playing the only instrument available to him, the banjo. He later became a fair dancer, and Bessie and he often partnered each other at the local dances.

Nevertheless, and in the most affectionate way, things radically altered with the arrival of John, her youngest brother. To say the least, family circumstances markedly changed. John was more boisterous and wilder than anyone had expected. To curb this energetic little boy, Bessie recalled that she had convinced him to join the Boy Scouts and as a bribe had bought him his first Cub cap and scarf. With his cap sitting crookedly on his head and the scarf untidily wrapped round his neck, and with the whole family looking on from the backroom window, he proudly marched up Dallfield Walk on his way, for the first time, to the Cub Scout Hall. It was as a Cub Scout that he was introduced to football, which became his lifelong passion. He would play the game at every possible opportunity, often to the neglect of his homework and meals.

He would often appear home from school for only a split second and, often with nothing to eat, dash off like greased lightning to Aylay Park, close to Wedderburn Street in the north of the city. Why? To play football of course. This passion lasted all through John's 79 years, first as a player, followed by refereeing, and finally as a spectator, until his death in 1990.

Football seemed to fill John's entire life; it certainly kept him out of trouble. The rest of the family hardly saw him except for a quick meal and bedtime, but they always knew where he was and what he was doing. In his enthusiasm for the game, all else was forgotten. He continually forgot about homework and repeatedly lost his school jotters. Bessie, who by then was in her teen years and working in the jute mills, was the one who dutifully replaced any of her young brother's losses.

John and my father (Sandy), who was his senior by some fourteen years, became great friends, being tied together by their undaunted support for one of the local football teams, Dundee United, but John was by far the more passionate. Sandy encouraged John, who had become quite an accomplished player and an even better goalkeeper. Despite his support for United, he was spotted by an agent for a neighbouring team, Arbroath Football Club, and was almost immediately signed up as a first team player. This was still a period of worldwide depression with little money available to spend, so such a signing was good financial news for John. However, it was short-lived as John had met his future wife, Betty.

Once married, they set up home in Campbell Street, Lochee, but within two decades, Britain soon found itself once again at war with Germany. John was called up just before his son was born; it would be five long, hostile years before he would see his one and only child, Steve, for the first time. John served his country as a private through the entire war and was part of Montgomery's Eighth Army. He fought through the deserts of North Africa, onto Sicily and the Italian mainland, then finally into Germany. He witnessed the eruption of Mt Vesuvius in 1944; even nature cried out against the suffering and carnage that humanity was inflicting upon itself. His only injury was one lost finger, which occurred when his armoured vehicle was attacked and destroyed in North Africa. Such injuries were regarded as minor, and once treated, he was sent back into the fray.

Demobbed in 1945, John returned home only to be unemployed for almost a year; however, he found work in Walker's jute mill in Lochee, where he remained until he retired. I remember him as a light-hearted, jovial person who once insisted that while in the desert he had not eaten for a week and was so hungry that he munched on his own finger. I, being too young to appreciate how ridiculous this was, casually asked, "Uncle John, what did it taste like?" His reply was swift and to the point. "It was bloody good," he said with a smile, waggling the remaining stump in front of me.

Once John had settled down after the war, he quickly realised that his days as a footballer were over, but this was not the end of his footballing career. Under guidance, mainly from my father, who already was an amateur referee, John was introduced to this alternative aspect of the game. During this refereeing phase, Sandy and John got into more trouble than at any other time in their lives. Sandy willingly passed many somewhat dubious pieces of advice and tips about refereeing down to his younger brother-in-law. It's true that mishaps often occurred in amateur refereeing, and to most referees, wrong venues, cancelled matches, and threats from players and spectators are all included, but the frequency of such incidents appeared to be disproportionately skewed against my uncle and father.

During these Saturday afternoons, the whole family would congregate in my grandparents' house on Dallfield Walk. There, my mother, with heart in mouth, anxiously awaited the safe return of her husband and brother. On their safe arrival, they would all sit round the kitchen table and listen to the most recent of sagas in the world of amateur refereeing. Often tears of laughter would run down their faces, all except that of my father, who was the master of droll storytelling. However, on one Saturday afternoon, Sandy appeared to be a bit agitated on his return home. It was John who recounted to the eagerly awaiting family the sequence of events that had taken place.

Both brothers-in-law were refereeing matches that were being played on adjacent pitches in the Aylay Park. John's watch had stopped just after the start of the second half. He reckoned that to stop such an evenly balanced match at this point would have caused too much disruption. So as Sandy's game had started just minutes before, John decided to guess when the final whistle should be blown; this was not a good idea. After Sandy had blown to end his game, John knew he had only minutes left, and the score was level at one goal each. But in the dying seconds, one side scored. However, according to some spectators of the now defeated team, John had overplayed the game by a few seconds. The defeated side and supporters were having none of this and quickly surrounded John in protest, demanding that the goal should be disallowed. My father, who was no stranger to disputes at the close of a football match, at first took little notice of the commotion and continued to finalise the details of his own game. But as things became more heated, he finally ran over to support John.

Just as he arrived at his brother-in-law's side, someone in the crowd punched John on the chest. Now John stood some five feet, eleven and weighed sixteen stone, and in those days, that was big. He was also very fit. He was not the type of man one would pick a fight with, but it was my five-feet-two-inch father who intervened, standing in front of John. He pulled out his whistle, which was on the end of a chain, and started to swing it as a threat to anyone who came near. Unfortunately, the chain was either longer than my father thought, or John's assailant was too close. No matter, the whistle bounced hard off the bridge of the assailant's nose. Blood immediately spurted out in all directions as he staggered back; a stunned silence of shock fell over the amassed crowd, and everything seemed to stop.

In that split second, both referees glanced at each other and then, with great speed and stealth, slipped through the lines of the hostile throng. By this time, followers of the triumphant team had formed an outer ring in support of the two referees, and they blocked the path of any would-be pursuers. This instantly led to hostilities between the opposing sides. Only after John and Sandy had created much space between themselves and the conflict did they look back, and they saw that much of Aylay Park had become a war zone. Soon after that, both retired, giving up their boots and whistles for the safer pastime of being spectators. Although my mother was glad that her husband and brother had given up what she regarded as a ridiculous afternoon's activity, she admitted that she missed the Saturday night banter and stories. And as my father often said, "It's only a game."

Voice from the Past

One Saturday afternoon while walking through the town centre with Meg, Bessie heard from behind a familiar voice. "Hello, Bessie." She turned, and there standing in front of her was Sandy, back from America. A coincidence? I wonder. He said that he had come back for her, but she, now some two years older, knew that was just male bravado. Although Bessie was extremely pleased to see him, she at first pretended not to be, asking why he didn't write. He then had to openly admit that he had forgotten her second name and did not want to write in case someone else received and read his letters. Some excuse! At first, Bessie appeared not to be amused and played hard to get. When he asked her out that night, she refused. "Why should I go out with someone who can't remember my name?" was her snubbing reply. He persisted and asked if he could take her out "tomorrow." At that point, Meg intervened. "Her name's Bessie McElroy." And then she said, turning to Bessie, "You're doing nothing tonight. Why don't you go out with the lad?" Which she did.

That was the moment when they became a couple, and if it were not for her good friend Meg Morris, it may never have happened.

Almost immediately they started dating on a regular basis. Bessie was 19 and Sandy 23 years old, and in those days, that was getting on for deciding who your lifelong partner would be, but it was still a few months before Bessie decided that he was the one she loved and wanted to marry. Once again, it was Meg who pointed out to her best friend that Sandy was a dependable and good man and that she could do a lot worse. After two years courtship, the couple were officially engaged and started to save and prepare for their wedding.

During their courtship, my folks not only danced; there was more to Dundee than just dance halls and jute mills; they also attended the movies, the local theatres, and music halls. One of the first venues they frequented was the 1933 purpose-built cinema house in the Murraygate, the La Scala (The Stairs). Also, in Castle Street, there was a small music and dance hall, the Theatre Royal. Although small and accessible by only a single staircase to the first floor, it was popular among the young. Of the theatres, my parents' favourite venues were Her Majesty's Theatre in the Seagate, the King's Theatre and Hippodrome in the Cowgate, and the Victoria Theatre in Victoria Road.

Her Majesty's Theatre was in the centre of town. This was live theatre at its best, where musicals, plays, and operas were all passionately attended by my mother, but my father was not quite so receptive. During the war, the theatre was converted into a cinema, the Majestic, which was more Sandy's cup of tea. Unfortunately, in 1941, this old theatre burnt down and lay as an empty derelict shell for many years. It was not until 1956 that it was rebuilt into the Capital Cinema; later it became a bingo hall then a restaurant and pub.

Since the burning down of Her Majesty's, it was the King's Theatre that assumed the city's live theatre legacy. In its heyday, it was a place regularly frequented by young couples, a popular venue due to the frequent appearance of many famous stars on its stage. These included Marie Lloyd (famous for the songs "Don't Dilly Dally on the Way" and "Oh! Mr Porter"), the singer and male impersonator Vesta Tilley, and of course Harry Lauder (later to become Sir Harry). Normally, such artists received a good reception from a receptive audience; however, one night this certainly did not apply to Harry Lauder.

During World War I, long before my parents had met and recalled by my father, Harry Lauder was appearing at the King's Theatre. In his great wisdom, he decided to make a patriotic speech during the evening performance. However, the audience were there to be entertained, not sermonised. They had had enough of nationalistic patriotism. "Give us a song, Harry!" was the call from the audience. Harry Lauder then passed a somewhat patronising and derogatory remark. The response was almost immediate. The audience jeered and booed until he left the stage, and he was not allowed back on. My father had never been all too fond of him, and especially after that fiasco. He once remarked, "He was always dressed up like an idiot. He made his money by trying to make a fool of his own folk."

The King's in 1929 became a full-time cinema, and by 1932 it was consumed into the Gaumont Film Group. However, it retained its old name and became, during the Second World War, a theatre for the forces, a Garrison Theatre. Although always referred to as the King's by my parents, it became known as the Gaumont in the 1950s and always retained a few weeks of reserved time for the arts (mainly ballet and opera). Then, in response to market forces, it deteriorated into a bingo hall and the Déjà Vu nightclub.

Another favourite theatre, which they attended as often as possible, was the Victoria, which had formerly been the Gaiety, in Victoria Road. While it was the Gaiety, it consisted of a small company, which was often bolstered by recruits from the local Hilltown area, and this continued after it changed name in 1910. Every kind of play and music hall entertainment was performed here. And my parents, during their courtship, were regulars; they knew that the best and most entertaining performances came during the late house on Friday. By that time, the entire cast had been paid and had had enough time to water themselves in the many local pubs. When the curtain was raised on each Friday evening's performance, no one in the audience, far less the cast, knew what was about to happen. The result was frequently an absolute hysterical fiasco, with actors forgetting their lines and improvising as they went along. Often, according to the amount of alcohol that had been consumed, petty jealousies and personal vendettas would leak out between impromptu lines of the actors, all on stage, all in front of an audience. Often, exchanged insults would become progressively more explicit, items were often thrown, and even fisticuffs ensued. It all added to the entertainment and was enthusiastically encouraged by the onlookers. Entrances and lines were repeatedly miscued, some stage entries lasted only a few seconds as the alcohol fuelled actor promptly fell off the stage, but somehow the show went on.

At the end of these frequently calamitous performances, the entire cast would manage, in the most elegant and individual way, to take their bow, only to continue hostilities after the final curtain had fallen. This was then followed by an ensuing week of eloquent performances from the same closely-knit band of actors, until the next Friday.

All the actors were thick-skinned and able to withstand the taunts of a Friday night audience, and they often gave as good as they got, which all added to the fun. It was claimed that if one could appear and survive on a Dundee stage, then one could survive any audience anywhere. Despite this, some locals with aspirations towards a stage career were always prime targets for hecklers. One such aspiring hopeful had acquired a small part in a long, dramatic Friday night performance. This well-known local lad had to face and address the audience and in a loud, inquisitive voice quote the lines "Where is my father?" This was a gifted opportunity for any audience, and answers came uncompromisingly fast from every part of the auditorium— and all with the same message. "He's in the Black Coo Bar up the Hull."[22] The hall went into a fit of hilarious uproar as the audience knew that that was exactly where his father was; the Black Cow was a pub on the Hilltown, not far from the theatre. Even the young actor was laughing as he stepped forward and said again in a loud voice,

---

[22] "He is in the Black Cow Bar on the Hilltown."

"He's afay proud o' me ye ken, me be'in an actor."[23] Again, the hall erupted, but this time it was with applause and cheers. "Good for you lad!" were the shouts, "Good for you!" The young man nodded and left the stage, having completed his small but memorable contribution to the drama.

Again, during the Friday evening's late house, there was an unforgettable husband and wife act. The wife had had a good drink beforehand and was desperate to appear sober on stage. What happened next was often recalled by my folks, always accompanied by tears of laughter running down their cheeks; it had been clearly etched on their minds from that moment. The wife muffed most of her lines, to the utter delight of the audience and dismay of the husband. The husband, however, did not bat an eyelid throughout the entire performance and spoke his lines with flawless precision, which made his now bedraggled wife sound even funnier, as her responses to her husband made no sense whatsoever. It was as if they had rehearsed the whole dramatic act as a comedy. At the end, as the curtain closed, they took their bow to great applause. Due to this apparent appreciation, the curtains reopened, but just that bit too soon. The husband had the wife by the throat and was attempting to throttle her. Realising that they were again on stage, and to cheers and laughter, they stopped, turned towards the audience, and both gave a most professional second bow in acknowledgement of the prolonged ovation.

These were great memories that Bessie and Sandy shared together, but alas nothing lasts forever. Just prior to the Second World War, in 1935, the Victoria became a cinema, so finally the curtain came down on this old theatre. These reminiscences are now only distant but cherished recollections in the maze of memories. How regrettable.

---

[23]   "He's very proud of me, you know, me being an actor."

CHAPTER 10

That's Life

The Pullar Family

Despite the religious differences, good will was always maintained between Bessie and her future father-in-law, William Pullar. Nevertheless, the Pullar family was a total contrast to that of the McElroy's. Steve McElroy, although just a jute worker, was employed in one of Dundee's choice trades; he was a carpetmaker employed in the Gilroy factory. He was an easy-going Catholic with a family of two sons and two daughters. His wife, who was a converted Catholic, had also been a jute worker.

Likewise, Sandy always seemed to keep Bessie's folks entertained, and they looked forward to his visits, which was a blessing in disguise; it maintained a balanced relationship between their respective families. However, despite mutual regard, the families never intermingled. But this religious mix and the relationship that Bessie had with her father-in-law tended to make the families more amenable to religious tolerance.

The father, William Pullar, who was long dead before I was born, was a much more severe individual and totally different from Steve, but not any better. The families were in sharp contrast to each other. William, a country-born lad, had become a police constable with the Dundee constabulary and had a reputation that went with it. An elder of the local Butterburn Protestant Church, he felt that he was an upright member of society responsible for setting an example to the community. His family had consisted of nine sons (no daughters), three of whom were lost during the Great War and a fourth having emigrated to Canada. The mother, Johanne, had a voice that was heeded and listened to by the father but in effect had little overall influence. The result was a family dominated from the father down, with Sandy, my father, unfortunately the youngest, firmly at the bottom of the pile.

Sandy's father was a born and bred countryman who was formidable, stern, and stubborn with his siblings. He was the youngest son of a farmer, Joseph Pullar, who farmed the Hillocks farm just north of the village of Burrelton, close to Coupar Angus. There, William worked and was brought up with the full intent of staying and taking over the farm; the oldest son had left earlier for New Zealand, under circumstances that were never talked about. However, as fate would have it, this was not to be as William met a girl, Johanne Miller, who would later become his wife. She lived in the small village of Kettins, again close to Coupar Angus, where she worked in the local jute factory. So, like my mother, she was a millworker. This, however, was not to the liking of the Pullar family, who would have much preferred William to have married a country lass who could help work the farm.

This family had been part of the rural scene in the Perthshire countryside for a long time. In fact, the first record of the family in Scotland was Henry Pullar. He was a Baillie of Perth, recorded in 1379. My great-great-grandfather was Joseph Pullar. He was a farmer at Kirkhill, Perthshire. He married Isabella Ramsay, and they had a daughter, Janet, and a son, Joseph. Janet died at the age of 21 on 4 October 1823. Joseph lived on to the right old age of 81, dying on 14 October 1886. His wife, Margaret Cross, did even better than her husband. She died in 1904 and had reached the age of 91, some achievement, especially in those days.

It was Joseph who took over the tenancy of the Hillocks farm. They had three daughters—Jessie, Isabella, and Marion—and a son, William. Jessie died relatively early, 11 December 1893. Isabella carried on until she was 84, until 24 January 1934. Marion, who reached the age of 83, had married Andrew Scott Findlay, who died, aged 79. They had only one daughter, Margaret, who carried on until 8 June 1990, passing away in Blairgowrie Cottage Hospital at the grand old age of 104. I had the honour of holding one of the cords as she was laid to rest in Cargill Churchyard Cemetery. A long-living family, especially for the women.

Cargill Cemetery, showing the Pullar headstones.

Attempted Murder, maybe?

However, the marriage between William and Johanne, despite all the objections, took place in the United Presbyterian Church in Coupar Angus on 22 April 1881, conducted by the Rev. Grainger. In due course, William left the farm, which meant that the family name had gone, and that marked the beginning of the end of the Pullar family in Burrelton and the Hillocks.

To keep the farm in the family, the couple start married life at the Hillocks, but that was certainly a mistake. It was not a happy period for the couple as from the start things went wrong. While there, Johanne was worked almost to the bone and life was made a complete hell by her two sisters-in-law. During her stay at the farm, this new wife took severe stomach pains that never seemed to get better. A doctor was never called despite her deteriorating condition. She alleged to her dying day that she was being slowly poisoned. Her new husband, William, although concerned, never dreamed that it was due to poisoning and thought it was just his wife adjusting to married life. However, eventually he did believe her and became extremely concerned, although he never actually accused the sisters of any wrongdoing. The newlyweds quickly moved out and found a rented flat in Dundee. It was in a tenement building (33 Cowgate), which is still there. As a result of the couple's action, William forfeited his inheritance, which was of little importance as his wife was now safe. Johanne's recovery was almost immediate, which clearly suggested that something was afoot at the Hillocks. Johanne never returned to the Hillocks and only occasionally did her husband, but their youngest sons certainly did. My father often recalled the times he had to work in the fields, especially during the long school holidays in summer. Young Sandy certainly had no holiday on the farm.

Being a strong farmer, William quickly found employment as a carter with the Caledonian Railway Company. Soon after which, in 1883, he joined the Dundee Police Force as an officer of the law, a job that well suited him. During his long association with the Dundee Police, he spent some twenty years on the harbour beat, which at that time was by no means a tranquil place. He remained in the police force until his retirement in 1920. William was a typical old-school policeman who was quick with his truncheon. He took no nonsense, and this was the case with his family of sons.

Johanne and William Pullar (the auld man).

The Pullars of the Hilltown

Of the sons, the highest-ranking and next in the family pecking order was named after his father, William (better known as Young Will). In those days, the firstborn son was normally named after the grandfather, but as there had been a family fall-out at the Hillocks farm regarding the marriage between Johanne and William, that privilege was not an option.

Young Will had the reputation of being a hypochondriac buying and investing in all the latest tablets and products that came onto the market. My mother recalled once suffering from an extremely bad headache, which was unusual for her to complain. From nowhere, this "walking chemist shop," Young Will, produced a wonder tablet to cure all headaches. It was an aspirin, which my mother had never heard of, but after cautiously consuming two of the tablets, the pain soon disappeared. She never thought that such a small tablet could be so effective; it was a miracle cure. Until then, one simply had to tolerate the most excruciating of pains; headaches, toothache, and back pain all had to be suffered. What a difference this made to everyday life.

Will regarded himself as a socialist; he was certainly a fine talker and prepared to take up the cause of any underdog. His brothers claimed that he could talk the "hind legs off a donkey." As far as his father, an ardent Tory, was concerned, his son's opinions were like a red rag to a bull. Both men would argue for hours about the politics of the day. My mother found this quite entertaining and informative; she was also convinced that both men were simply winding the other up, as they appeared to display no malice whatsoever towards each other. Young Will was a very amiable person, good-humoured, who rarely made a fuss. This was similar in many respects to my own father, which was probably the reason they left for America together despite an age gap of almost twenty years.

Of all the nine sons, Will was probably the most studious, and on his return home, he trained and became a technical teacher. For the rest of his working life, he taught in Dundee's Graham Street Junior Secondary School. He had resettled in Carnoustie, and there, after a few years, met and married a local lass, Mary Cable, whom he remained with for the rest of his life. Mary had been a member of a locally famous musical family act (the Cable Family); she was also a music hall and old silent movie pianist, all of which carried the shadowy suspect of non-respectability. However, Mary also held the highly distinguished position of resident organist in Carnoustie's Old Parish Church; prior to this, she was organist in Maxwell's Town and Downfield Baptist churches, both in Dundee, and later the Old Abbey Church in Arbroath, followed by the Panbride Church near Carnoustie. Such esteemed credentials reinforced her image of propriety. Even after Will's death, and during the frequent visits of my parents to Carnoustie, Mary would entertain us by playing the piano and reminisce about her nostalgic bygone music hall and silent movie days.

John (or Jock) was the next brother. My mother never met this brother as he and his wife had emigrated to Canada before my parents met. They had one girl, Audrey, and two boys, William, and Vincent. Jack was a locomotive fireman and travelled across this vast continent. Unfortunately, while passing through the Rocky Mountains, a bridge had collapsed prior to his crossing and the whole train length careened over a precipice, taking Jack and many others to their death. His son, Vincent, was then left to carry on the family name.

During the Second World War, Vincent was recruited into the Canadian St Margaret's Light Infantry and transported to Britain. While on leave, he managed to spend some time with his long-lost Dundee family, living at the Hilltown address with his grandparents. It was there my mother met him for the first time. She said that she was surprised to find this big, good-looking soldier in her mother-in-law's living room. She of course did not know who he was, but he recognised her immediately. Johanne had sent a photograph of Bessie and her family to their Canadian relatives, and it had been placed on the mantlepiece back home. He was an extremely friendly person and visited my folks in Alexander Street each day of his three-day visit. William, my brother, who was only about 10 years old (I was not yet on the scene), was fascinated by his new-found older cousin, who told him about life in Canada. It was wartime, and the family only had their rations to share with Vincent, but they did their best. After his three-day visit round the family, he returned to his regiment, which was then sent off to Normandy and on through Europe. The family never heard from him again. After the war, my mother wrote to Canada, but there was no reply.

Robert (Bob) was another of the brothers Bessie never met. He married a girl called Agnes Steele, and they had two girls, one of whom died while still an infant. Bob never lived to see his surviving daughter grow up as he was killed in the Great War. Agnes remarried and moved to the Fife village of Coatbridge; nevertheless, my folks kept in touch with her and frequently visited. There was another two brothers that Bessie had never met, David (Dave) and Frederick (Fred). She knew little about them other than David had two boys and a girl and Fred was another one who lost his life in the Great War; his body was never found. However, my father regarded Fred as his favourite brother, and he was the one he missed most. He told me that often Fred would slip him a penny or two for some chore or message he would run.

Fred with young Sandy. Fred fell in France, 1915.

Of the surviving brothers, Joseph (Joe) was the next. He was often referred to as "Boss" as he held a position of foreman with the town council. He and his wife, Jessie, had a son (Joseph) and a daughter (Jessie). Their other son, William, reached manhood but early in his young life, he suffered from a heart attack and died. However, Jessie married Jack Jones, an upholsterer to trade, and they had two daughters, Diana, and Cynthia.

Next in line among the brothers was George. He was a butcher and had his own shop on the Hilltown, just opposite the family home. According to the rest of the brothers, he had the reputation of being a bit grippy with money. My mother recalled one Friday afternoon just before she started cleaning her mother-in-law's house, which she dutifully did each week. The rest of the family was out, and Johanne, with a raw smile on her face, beckoned to Bessie, "Come here and look at this." My mother could always tell when Johanne was up to something. They both went into the back bedroom, which had become the sole property of George. Johanne produced what could only be described as a pile of old rags. "Is this for the ragman?" asked Bessie. "No" was the reply. "It's George's underwear." Both women could hardly believe what they were looking at. As Bessie held these bits of cloth up to the light, she could only see large holes in what were supposed to be his long johns and vests—in fact, in every piece of underwear he had. Johanne sighed. "There's mare holes than anything else and it's no as if he's nay money." Bessie as usual started to giggle. "What a pair sowl ga'in aboot like that, if only his customers knew what he hid on underneath."[24] They both started laughing. "I'll ge yi money and awa up ti Smith and Horners an' get him some new breeks."[25] Bessie threw the old rags out on her way to Smith and Horners, a clothier on the Hilltown, where she bought a few sets of men's underwear. The women were like partners in crime, the only two in the whole world, other than George, who knew about his underwear—but not for long.

His new clothes were placed on top of his bed ready for him coming home from work. By the time he came in from his butcher's shop, the whole family knew of the underwear fiasco and, of course, were sitting in the living room in silence. George was immediately aware of the quiet atmosphere in the room and knew that something was afoot. He was often the butt of his brother's jokes due to his penny-pinching thriftiness, "What's wrang?" he asked. No one spoke. He was not surprised as this was often the response when he was being set up. He walked suspiciously into his room, which he had selfishly assumed as his own despite the other brothers having to share. There followed a silence as all waited in anticipation. Then

---

[24] "What a poor soul having to walk about like that. If only his customers knew what he had on underneath."

[25] "I'll give you money and go up to Smith and Horners and buy him some new long johns."

came the eruption— "What's a this then?"—as George stamped into the living room. "Ah wisni needin awny underwear!"[26] This was followed by hoots of laughter from the rest of the family, including Bessie and the father. "Away yi dafty" was his mother's reply. "Wir yi tyin ti make a fale o' us, what if yi hid an accident, an yi had ti tack yir clays aff?"[27] George's voice went up an octave. "Am no payin fir this." This went on for ages, with the house in a state of hysterical uproar as he persistently insisted that he was not paying for the clothes. However, on learning that it was Bessie who had gone for the purchase, he calmed down. Bessie could do no wrong in his eyes so reluctantly he agreed to pay up. Bessie was told that her brother-in-law always had this commotion when he needed something new; he just would not spend the money.

There was another incident weeks later when George displayed his true thrifty colours. Bessie noticed one day in her in-law's house that George had no socks on. "Whar's yir socks, George?" Bessie asked as she looked down at his feet. "On ma feet" was the reply. At this, he unashamedly lifted his trouser legs, and sure enough, the rest of his socks were there round his ankles, but nothing on his feet. He even had suspenders holding the rest of the socks up. "Ah well, nabody will ken when ma shoes are on"[28] was his excuse. She later learnt that he would search under the beds of his brothers and collect all their old shoes. He would then look for two that matched, which he would wear before buying himself a new pair.

Being older than my father, he always felt that he knew better, which caused some amusing animosity, at least to my mother, between them. She recalled being pregnant with me and how apparently concerned George was about my welfare. In fact, he was in an awful state to such an extent that my father angerly reported to my mother that George had given him a ticking off for making her pregnant.

---

[26] "I wasn't needing any underwear."
[27] "Were you trying to make a fool of us? Suppose you had had an accident and you had to take your clothes off."
[28] "Ah well, nobody will notice when my shoes are on."

"Getin' yir wife in a state like that, what were yi thinking? The wumans nearly forty." In fact, he was right. My mother was forty when I was born, and in those days that was getting on to be having children. However, it was unfair for my father's brother to rile him like that as he was even more worried. He was only too aware of his wife's miscarriage a few years before, when their twin girls were lost. He would often angrily remark, "Yi wid think he wis the father the wye hs's kerryin on.[29]"

Not surprisingly, George remained a bachelor until his fifties, when he married a spinster lady, Margaret Kidd (Peggy). This certainly changed him somewhat, and for the better. The couple of course had no children, but they both readily agreed to become my godparents, even promising to take care of me if anything happened to my mother, Bessie. This seemed to be in total disregard as to what my father's intensions were. However, as my godfather, George once gave me a threepenny piece (old money), which was an unusual act to say the least, so with great reverence it was placed on the mantlepiece. It then, apparently in an act of its own doing, fell through a small gap down into the back of the fireplace. It never of course crossed George's mind to replace it with another.

While on that subject, I recall the case of George's wedding gift to the local children, told to me by my father. In those days, it was customary, when departing by taxi for attendance at a wedding, for money to be thrown out to the awaiting and expectant crowd of children. From far and wide, these children always managed to hear of a pending wedding and promptly appeared at any such event. My father, who was the best man to his brother, threw copper coins from one side of the taxi. The groom, George, did similar at the other side as they left for the church. Now George always kept his copper coins in one pocket and his silver coins in another. However, being an excitable man, he forgot which pocket held the copper coins, and in his temporarily confused state, he went into the wrong pocket and threw out £2 worth of silver. There was an immediate melee of kids

---

[29] "You would think that he was the father, the way he's carrying on."

scrambling and fighting for the money. George immediately realised his error and could not let it go. He stopped the taxi and ran back. "Come on, lads. Play fair. That was a mistake!" he was shouting. This fell on deaf ears, and within seconds, he was left standing alone. The kids had gone, and so had his money.

One of the contrasting figures in the family, and probably the one my father most resembled, was my uncle Jim. He was the second youngest of the brothers and the exact opposite to George. He was one of the most easy-going men I have ever met. He was droll and often very funny, and nothing seemed to bother him. A good plumber but not too fond of work, he spent much of his time in his parents' house and not at his trade. This behaviour annoyed my father; nevertheless, in his brother's defence, he often remarked that this didn't really matter as he was a council worker, which doesn't say much for the council's Works Department. However, Jim's droll sense of humour certainly made up for it.

His wife, Jane Hunter, was already known to my mother. Jane, who for some unknown reason was called Jean, was twelve years older than Bessie and worked in her father's bakery on the Hilltown. There, every Sunday morning, Bessie would be sent for scones to the Hunters' bakery, where she would envy Jean behind the counter with her father and two sisters, never realising that later in life they would become sisters-in-law. Jean would regularly slip an extra couple of scones into Bessie's bag, so there was an early bond between them. This bond lasted throughout Jean's lifetime, and it was my mother who sat at her bedside until the end, dying at the age of 82. They had a daughter, young Jean, who went on to be a teacher of physical education. She married, leaving Dundee to live in Glasgow with her husband, Dr James Moncur.

My parents and I (as a small boy) would occasionally drop in on Jim and his wife for a social visit. Jean was a quiet, reserved person, unlike her husband, but she and Bessie got on well and she was always glad to see us. As usual, the adults finished the evening with a game of cards. This was an opportunity for Jim to come into his own. To play cards with him was an experience and meant that one simply had to take things as they came. Jean was never quite able to do this; I don't think that she fully understood her husband's sense of humour. He would hide cards up his sleeves or under the table, and of course Sandy would encourage him. The whole episode was a piece of fun, and by just watching I was kept amused for the entire evening. Unfortunately, Jean never saw this, and the evening always finished up in a fall-out between husband and wife, which to me was even more amusing than the card games. Jean would inevitably threaten to leave him and come home with us. Of course, she never did – thank goodness. Come the end of the night, they would be standing together, pals once again, waving us goodbye till the next time. He and my father were close. They even looked alike, and often my mother would state that she had to look twice to see which one was which. Their nature was also similar, but my father was the harder worker.

The Pullar family, 1899.

Holiday of a Lifetime, Perhaps

Despite the hard times, there were still fond memories that my parents held onto well into their old age; one of the most memorable was their time at the Hillocks farm. This was the deciding event that brought them permanently together as a single united couple.

During the Dundee holiday week, they were both invited to the Hillocks for a holiday. William told the couple that the holiday was free, and they would be most welcome, but as he spoke those memorable words, there was a wry, cynical smile on his wife's face. The young couple felt as if they were ambassadors for the Dundee branch of the family as things were still strained between Johanne and the two farm sisters. Bessie, the eternal optimist, felt that things may be memorable although not as dramatic as her mother-in-law had experienced.

First was the bus journey to Coupar Angus, followed by a rough horse-and-carriage ride to the village of Burrelton. However, from there on, the road was waterlogged so they had to walk the rest of the journey to the farmhouse, a distance of at least one mile. This was up a steep incline to the front door where they arrived wet, with sodden shoes, and exhausted. There they received a rather muted welcome at first, as the family thought that they would not be coming due to the rain. Nevertheless, they were fed and shown to their respective rooms, Bessie sharing a bed with one of the sisters, which she was used to with her own sister. However, that night, Bessie could not sleep due to continuous knocking in the attic above. She had been told that this was just storage space, so no one was there. It was a bit frightening: who or what could it be? Eventually, the sister woke and sleepily said, as she turned over, "It's only the rats. They live up there, but they'll not come down. The windows are shut." At that, Bessie hid under the covers, and with all sorts of outrageous thoughts passing through her mind listened, for the rest of the night, to the thumping noise of the rodents above as they scurried back and forth.

Next morning, bedraggled and tired due to lack of sleep, she sat down at the long kitchen table and was presented with her one and only breakfast option, a cold piece of porridge that had been stored in what was called the porridge drawer. Seemingly, countryfolk made porridge only once per week, poured it into a kitchen draw, and took a slice each morning as required. On the other hand, at least the tea was hot. Things got worse when she discovered that Sandy, who was nowhere to be found, had received a breakfast of bacon and eggs (in fact two eggs). Much later, she learnt that this was because she was not family and therefore was not entitled to such a privilege. To add insult to injury, the sisters handed her a scrubbing brush and asked if she would help by scrubbing the kitchen table, which she resentfully did. Bessie was kept busy every day while Sandy was either visiting or playing football. The only time they had together was after five o'clock in the evening.

Come Friday, she again was handed the scrubbing brush, but this time she was told that it was her turn to scrub the table and then the kitchen floor. They then enlightened her of the fact that they had decided she was to take over a stall at the village fete on Saturday morning. Bessie's good nature had been tested to breaking point. She thought that she was to be a guest in their home, but it was clear that the guest status did not apply to her; she was expected to work for her keep. She politely handed back the scrubbing brush and explained that although she was willing to help, if they were ever invited to Dundee for a short holiday, they would be welcomed as guests and would not be expected to work for their board. That evening, she told Sandy that she had had enough. "Come on then, let's just go" was his reply. He knew that Bessie had been worked hard. He had protested, but the sisters simply ignored him. He remembered the days when he was a schoolboy sent out to the Hillocks farm for the full summer holiday, where he had to work from morning till the darkness fell at night; he too was ready to leave.

They were fully packed first thing next morning. The sisters knew that this would get back to their brother in Dundee and he would not be pleased, so a great fuss was made to try to keep them at the farm, but the couple was adamant and left. It was raining heavily so the fete had been cancelled. *Good. Serves them right* Bessie thought. They walked the mile from the farmhouse into Burrelton, where they caught the first bus into Perth, and from there, home to bonnie Dundee. The rain was so heavy that their suitcase became saturated and burst open, but that didn't matter. They were free, they had stood up for themselves, and they felt that they had struck their first blow together.

Once home, their first port of call was to the Hilltown and Sandy's parents. Met at the door by his mother, Johanne, she was not at all surprised at their premature departure from the farm; she had lasting memories of her own. By this time, all the anger and frustration had gone from the pair, which was good as they were now ready to talk calmly. The four sat down over a cup of tea. "Well, how did you get on?" William asked.

Of course, it was Bessie who did most of the talking, but by this time, her sense of humour had clicked in and nothing serious came out. It all reduced into a series of hysterical stories. For the rest of the evening, the four sat round the fire and exchanged stories and experiences about the Hillocks and its occupants, and there was a lot to tell.

That night, Bessie felt that she had truly become one of the family. Even the old man, William, was laughing and sharing little family stories from the past. Johanne would periodically punctuate the conversation and say, still in her Coupar Angus twang, "I kent this wid happen, I telt yi."[30] She felt that her own experiences at the Hillocks farm had now been vindicated and had not been in her own imagination.

---

30   "I knew this would happen. I told you."

Sandy and Bessie on holiday, Blairgowrie.

Religious Differences

Bessie's father-in-law, William, had the reputation of being a cantankerous and irritable old man who did not wish to listen to any opinion other than his own. On the other hand, she was close to her own father, Steve, and in many ways, they were similar. He was a well-liked, amicable person and thoroughly respected by all who knew him. In addition, he was a Catholic (as was Bessie) and was a completely contrasting figure to that of the father-in-law. Such distinctions made the warm relationship that developed between Bessie and her father-in-law all the more surprising. But she was the only one who was able to talk him round to see things her way.

William looked upon her as the daughter he never had, and they would often sit together over cups of tea and have long conversations about everything and nothing. The "auld man" (as he was respectfully called, mind you, not to his face) turned out to be not nearly as stubborn as was first thought. They remained close friends until his death at 78.

Moreover, she befriended all the in-laws, and that included the daughters-in-law, who seemed to trust Bessie; there was no apparent animosity regarding her special relationship with the "auld man." In fact, they appeared to welcome it, as it took much tension out of family affairs. When Bessie was around, this obstinate man became a far more pleasant and amenable person.

Sandy's father would display his likeness for Bessie in many strange ways. Once during the young couple's courtship, they decided to holiday in Perth (only twenty-two miles up the River Tay) for a week. In those days, that was quite an event as not many couples went on holiday, especially if they were unmarried. The auld man was particularly anxious and genuinely concerned for Bessie's well-being while in the care of his son. So much so that it involved him and his wife, Johanne, seeing them off at the rail station. There, he surprised everyone when he forced a half crown (around twenty-five pence) into my mother's hand. He was regarded, within the family, as being "fell grippy" with his money, and a gesture of this magnitude, especially to a potential daughter-in-law, was unheard of.

However, despite the inroads made by my mother into the Pullar family, there existed a religious divide; the Pullar side was staunchly Protestant whereas the McElroys were equally staunch Catholics, and in those days, that could have been an unsurmountable obstacle to any promising relationship. Nevertheless, Bessie's affable and cordial personality had so affected and captivated auld man Pullar that religion no longer became an issue.

Also, on the McElroy side, her mother (Mary Macdonald), on her marriage to Steve, had converted to Catholicism, so she understood her daughter's situation only too well. Although Mary had taken the belief of her husband, she was not a totally won-over Catholic and was quite in agreement with Bessie's decision. The father, Steve, took a little more convincing, but he liked his future son-in-law and followed his wife's lead. Years later, with a rare smile, Mary admitted to her daughter that she had never had any intensions to attend chapel. "I jist went ti the religious classes ti get Steve."[31]

Naturally, this was not all one-sided, and Protestant Sandy had tried to become interested in his future wife's Catholic belief, which spectacularly failed. He even attended mass with Bessie, but once was enough, even for Bessie. It was in St Mary's Chapel, Forebank, and as they walked under the large and impressive Roman arched doorway, Bessie blessed herself at the stone font, set to one side in the doorway. Sandy did the same, and together they walked into the chapel. This was the first time he had been inside a Catholic church and was guided entirely by his girlfriend—what she did, he copied.

During the service, a collection plate was passed around, into which Bessie duly placed her offering. At this point, Sandy looked a bit confused and nudged his girl. "How many collections do they have here?" he whispered. "Just one" was the quick and quiet reply. "Well, I've already paid my money in the plate at the front door. It cost me a bob." There was a pause from Bessie, who then turned and looked at him with a big beaming smile. "Yi dafty, that's no a collection plate. That was the holy water. You're meant to bless yourself with it." "Well, can I get my money back on the way oot?" She then nudged him and putting her fingers to her lips said, "Shoosh, or you'll get us thrown oot." They nudged each other and quietly giggled throughout the rest of the mass.

After the service, they both raced to Dallfield Walk, where Bessie through continued laughter explained to her parents what Sandy had done. They had been keenly awaiting the outcome of the young couple's adventure, and they were not disappointed. After listening to the story, Steve placed his arm over his future son-in-law's shoulder. "I think it'll be a Protestant wedding after all, son. I don't think you're cut out to be a Catholic," he said laughingly.

---

[31] "I just went to the religious classes to get Steve."

Sandy had a good sense of humour. He needed it as he was ribbed about the holy water episode for weeks. This was particularly amusing to Mary, who had been a Protestant and was quick to point out that Sandy paid to get into the chapel and then had to pay to get out.

Both families appeared to be respectful towards each other's beliefs. If things were left as they were, then all would have been well, but that rarely happens in real life. As soon as Bessie declared her intent to become Protestant and stand alongside her future husband, the reaction from the Catholic priests could only be described as outrageous. Night after night, priests and nuns visited Bessie at home, or after mass. They harassed her with arguments and threats as an attempt to overwhelm her into changing her mind. Once a Catholic, always a Catholic was the main thrust of their argument, and when such silly reasoning had little effect on this determined woman, they resorted to even greater threats. She would go to hell, her marriage would not be recognised by God, and in God's eyes, her children would be illegitimate. These words greatly upset not only Bessie but her whole family. Her mother had never experienced such shocking behaviour from the Protestant Church when she changed, in the opposite direction, to become Catholic.

Things came to a head when Steve, after a week of hard work, returned home one Friday night. Wanting nothing more than a peaceful evening in front of the fire, he was instead confronted in his own living room by his daughter in floods of tears and the local priest holding court on the wrongs of Protestantism. This was too much; his wife had been a Protestant and had changed to become a somewhat reluctant Catholic, and he certainly did not want a second grudging believer in the family. He also understood and sympathised with his daughter's dilemma. Steve was a faithful Catholic, but his daughter's happiness was paramount to him and no priest would interfere with that. This was an unacceptable intrusion into a family affair. Bessie told me that she had never seen her father so angry. He ordered the priest out of the house, which was an unheard-of act of defiance against the Catholic Church; he then turned to his daughter and apologised to her for not having put a stop to this harassment sooner.

Next day, Saturday, he rose early and walked to St Mary's Chapel; there, he explained to the ecclesiastics that his eldest daughter had listened to their opinions and advice and had made up her own mind. He insisted that they now leave her alone as that their continued persistence was becoming a nuisance. This did not go down well, but the chapel adhered to his wishes.

Bessie that same year converted and duly became a Protestant.

Setting up Home

However, it still took a year of painstaking search before they at last found a house to rent. She told me that finding a place of their own was one of the most satisfying and thrilling highlights of her life. For months they both had toured around every housing factor in the city, asking, almost begging, that they be given the keys to a flat, any flat anywhere, but all was in vain.

One hot Saturday morning in late July, while trekking from one housing factor to the next, Bessie decided to try the factors at the bottom of the Wellgate (Shepherd). She had not visited them for a whole week. Walking into the office and expecting the same answer she had heard so often, "Nothing today, sorry," she was stunned into absolute speechlessness when handed a key. It was a top-storey flat in Alexander Street. The office girl had seen this reaction before and smiled. "Yes, it's yours, if you want it." "We want it all right," Bessie nervously replied, accepting the key. She then dashed out of the office and up the Hilltown to her future mother-in-law, where Sandy had just returned home from working overtime. The words could hardly come out when they met. "We have a key. We have a key," she repeated excitedly. She could not remember where, but there on the label was the address: 130 Alexander Street. It was theirs.

The tenement still stands today.

The tenement: top flat, fourth from left and
right of the gargoyle figureheads.

That afternoon, they viewed the house and Sandy signed for it.
Women always needed a man's signature for any transaction in those
days. Bessie then told her own folks, who were just as excited. They
rushed up to see the young couple's first home. It was a two-roomed
bunt-n-ben, like their own, and in bad need of decoration; the floor
covering, which was a valuable commodity, had been lifted by the
relatives of the previous tenant, who had died. The walls were dirty
with a thick, grease-like film, especially over the area beside an old
cast iron gas cooker. The wallpaper throughout the house was torn
as if an aborted attempt had been made to strip it from the walls.
If possible, the roof was even dirtier than the walls, due to the gas
mantle fitment above the mantelshelf. Gas was their only form of
lighting, and it gave off a vapour when lit, forming a black ring above
the fixture. It was not until 1938 that my folks had electricity installed
into the flat. It cost the grand total of £2-7/6p (around £2.87).

The windows were also affected. So blackened were they that
one could not see through them, but this was due more to neglect
than gas vapour. Also, there was a draughty front door that leaked

when raining; it opened onto an open landing (a plat) with a set of half-high railings. A game that we played as children was to slip in and out of the railing bars. Or often we would sit on top of the cross bars and, with only our feet holding onto the vertical spars, lean as far back as we could, something for which I received a good hiding from my father. He patiently waited until I had performed this most dangerous of acts and then in a flash grabbed me and pulled me into the house. I never attempted such a stupid trick again. The only thing that prevented a fifty-foot drop down into the back green were those railings.

As the couple viewed their future home, these disparagements became redundant when they realised the most important features of the house: an inside toilet had been installed. This was something that neither one had been brought up with; both had outside toilets shared by other tenants.

Looking out of the back window onto North Ellen Street, gargoyles could just be seen on each side of next door's windowsill, and they're still there. These were probably the houses reserved for the original supervisors and gaffers of the mills, not for underlings like my family. In a later rumoured story, these figures had by far a more interesting origin. It involved two brothers who ran a building company that was commissioned to build the tenements on behalf of the jute baron family Grimond, who in turn rented these flats out to their employees, thus tightening the grip on their workforce. This was a feature of the nineteenth century, when there was a great influx of people into the city from the surrounding countryside, all believing in the illusion of a better life in the false utopia of the Dundee jute mills. Each respective brother built a tenement block on the opposite sides of North Ellen Street. However, in time, a feud broke out between the two men, and it was this dispute that led to one of the brothers attaching the gargoyles to his side of the street, thus making crude faces at his brother's building. There is no credence to this strange tale other than the story itself and of course the gargoyles.

For my folks, the following months were filled with great activity and excitement as they hastily decorated and furnished the flat and of course arranged for their wedding. They were married on 19 December 1930. Their wedding took place in the Albany Terrace Manse. It was conducted by the Rev Hugh Hutcheson, and the reception was in the Union Hall, 69 Nethergate. They remained happily married for fifty-two years, until my father's death on 11 January 1982, at the age of 82.

My parent's wedding day, with bridesmaid
Grace and best man George.

CHAPTER 11

The Best-Laid Plans

Married Life

The Pullar family tended to be hard on the daughters-in-law, perhaps due to there being only sons in the family—nine in total. A large family was the norm in those days, but a family with nine sons and no daughters, along with a stubborn retired policeman as a father-in-law was unusual. Bessie, being the most recent of the female in-laws, was expected to carry out certain tasks for her new mother-in-law and, being young and unfamiliar with such expectations, agreed. Admittedly, Sandy did ask his wife if she would agree to such tasks, and credulous Bessie regarded them as a challenge. Each Friday evening, after a full day's work in the mills (and with her own house to look after), she would clean the in-laws' house from top to bottom, which included scrubbing floors, cleaning brasses, and blackening their large, cast iron grate (fireplace), a very undesirable task. While she was pregnant with her son, William, she dutifully carried out her now expected duties, with little thanks or payment.

In later years she often reflected on how foolish she had been, stating that she should have copied the other daughters-in-law. They were older and less gullible than Bessie and had already refused to perform any burdens expected by the mother-in-law. Female fallouts within the family were regular occurrences, which meant that the womenfolk became exempt from any presumed duties. This meant that Bessie was left with the lot. Of course, Sandy did not get off with impunity. He was expected to attend to his father's vegetable plot, situated on the slopes of the Dundee Law. During the summer months, he spent most Sunday afternoons hard at work digging, planting, and reaping the produce.

A normal Sunday for my parents, at the allotment.

Despite this, things were looking up for the family. My parents complemented each other's personality, and they rarely disagreed with each other; well, let us rephrase that. My father rarely disagreed with his wife, leaving most of the family decisions to her. Although my father was well liked, with a mulled, droll sense of humour, he was the more serious and cynical of the two. My mother, the eternal optimist, would tent to giggle and see the funny side of life.

The Sosh

One such decision made by Bessie, like many other housewives in those days, was to become a member of the Co-operative Society (more commonly known as the "Sosh"). She was in the Dundee Eastern branch (DECS). The co-operative had stores over the whole country. And as the housewives purchased their weekly messages from their nearest Sosh, they also bought shares in the company, which then paid out an annual cash dividend ("the divi").

My brother William (or Bill), the first grandson in the family, was, as was the custom, named after his paternal grandfather. (I was named after my father, Alexander.) Bill was the first grandson on both sides of the family, so a great fuss was made when this ten-pound baby boy arrived on Saturday 31 October 1932. My mother's sister, May, was delighted at becoming an aunt and made frequent unexpected visits to the house just to see her new-born nephew. After a few months, Bessie found a part-time job as a receptionist with Hyde, the dentist. This was convenient as it was in the centre of town. Whilst at work, her mother took care of the baby, and it became the job of the now Uncle John to carry Bill from Dallfield Walk to Alexander Street each night for his sister.

A Tragedy in the Family

The culmination came one Friday evening. It was a few years before the start of the Second World War and Bessie had once again become pregnant. With a heavy cold and late into her pregnancy, she appeared at the in-laws' house, ready to dutifully carry out her duties. Clearly unwell, she then, in the rain, walked home. My father, who was of the same Pullar family ilk, did not appear to see anything wrong in this practice and was oblivious to the fact that his wife was clearly unwell.

The next day, at home, she had a miscarriage and lost her twin girls. My mother was a hardy woman and recovered quickly, but it devastated her, and no one appeared to understand. Certainly, the mother-in-law, Johanne, neither accepted nor understood the underlying cause of the miscarriage tragedy and expected Bessie to promptly resume her duties. After a short period of time, she even asked her son when his wife would be resuming her cleaning obligations. Perhaps she had become immune to such an event, having lost a few children of her own at childbirth. The whole Pullar family appeared to be prepared to allow her to pick up where she had left off. Even my father one day suggested that it was perhaps time she thought about returning to her in-law tasks. Bessie's reaction and answer to this was short and sweet; she had no intentions to return to the Friday night status quo. In fact, she had no intensions of returning to the in-laws' house again. Sandy eventually sided with his wife. She had been through enough and had done far more than any other daughter-in-law, enduring great suffering for it.

An air of discontent continued for over a year, then from seemingly nowhere, Sandy was summoned by his father to meet him one Saturday morning and to wear his suit with collar and tie. He had no idea why, but it was his father's request and seemed to be important, so Sandy adhered to the request and met his father.

The two men walked for a while, the father setting the pace, until they came to the door of the Dundee Savings Bank at the corner of Stirling Street and the Hilltown. There, at the door, William explained that if he died first, before his wife, Johanne, then the family estate may not be equally divided among the remaining sons. He knew that his wife was easily influenced by certain members of the family and that Sandy and Bessie may be squeezed out of any rightful inheritance. "I'm makin' sure you and a'n yir wife Bessie get yir share before I dei. There are too muny greedy hans in this outfit."[32]

This turned out to be all too true. Bessie's father-in-law had recognised the sacrifice she had made, and this was a small token of thanks, and remorse. The two men entered the bank and Sandy received his first bank book, into which his father had deposited £100. An hour later, Sandy arrived home, where Bessie was nervously waiting. "What was that a' about?" she asked anxiously, thinking that something was wrong in the family. "There, hay a look at that, wife," he said, handing over the book. This was a fortune in those days, and Bessie remained speechless for a few minutes.

Then she blurted out all in the same breath, "I thought there was something wrang wi' yir mither, or ane o' yir brithers, but I never thought this. I hope yi thanked yir father."[33] Sandy laughed. "I did that, wife. The auld man said that it was up to us how we spend it." My grandfather must have known that the end was near, as not long after that, the auld man died. But he had made sure that Bessie and Sandy had received their share of his inheritance. Still, within my mother's heart, this sincere gesture could not compensate for her lost daughters.

Nevertheless, once the couple realised that this money was theirs, they sat down and started to plan how best to use this small fortune. Sandy had recently been made idle, and Bessie was only working part-time in Brown's tobacconist shop at the foot of the Hilltown, so this money was a godsend to the family. Bessie saw that the money lasted for years and helped them through some tough times. She budgeted so well that the family went on a week's holiday each summer; they would depart Dundee and vacate to such exotic places as Blairgowrie, Perth, and even Buckhaven in Fife (all within thirty miles of their hometown).

---

[32] "I'm making sure you and your wife, Bessie, get your share before I die. There are too many greedy hands in this family."

[33] "I thought there was something wrong with your mother, or one of your brothers, but I never thought this. I hope you thanked your father.

From the Sosh dividend, and the money from Sandy's father, the couple managed to buy a double-sprung settee with matching chairs (a three-piece suite), which Bessie had long admired in the co-operative furniture store window in the Seagate. She would proudly point out to all visitors to their home. "The arms are double sprung." Sandy took a little convincing about such a large purchase, but she quickly pointed out that the suite was not really that stated price, as she would receive a cash dividend on the purchase at the end of the financial year. She then cautiously explained that the settee could act as a bed for the arrival of any later ones to come. Whether my father agreed with the logic behind this large financial outlay, I don't know, but despite being more grippy than my mother, he accepted his wife's wishes and went along with them.

Despite my mother's job being only part-time, it was a financial blessing for the family, especially while my father was idle, and like the rest of the Dundee workforce, that was often. Nevertheless, things appeared to be working out for the couple, and they even started to plan for a larger family. The money that was left in the bank was conveniently held there for what my mother called "a rainy day." And there were many rainy days ahead when that money was needed to keep the family financially afloat.

The Co-operative Society was regarded by many Dundonians as an essential part of their daily lives; the cash dividend that was periodically paid out acted as a savings bank for large items, including school clothes and even holidays. I well remember, as a little boy, playing in the sawdust-covered floor of the local Sosh store, in Ann Street, while my mother purchased her weekly shopping. For me, this was the Saturday routine; it was always the same. On returning home from the morning movie matinee in the Plaza Picture House on the Hilltown, my mother would write into her official Sosh shopping book the family's weekly list of groceries. Together we would walk to the store, and I, of course, was in expectation of my usual two-ounce bag of doll mixtures. Once in the store, she placed her book into a small slot in the top of a box, which was just large enough for the customers' books to be stored together, one on top of the other.

Eventually, the book would be recovered by a shop assistant through a similar slot on the reverse side at the bottom of the box. This was a perfect method of maintaining first in, first served, and it meant that there was no dispute as to who was next. The women then sat on the wooden benches and chattered among themselves while the accompanying kids played in the sawdust-covered floor. Often, I would wander over to the sweetie counter and then look across to my mother, who would deliberately avoid any eye contact. I was making sure that she had not forgotten to mark in the two ounces of dolly mixtures. I often watched the assistant at the butter and cheese counter skilfully use a thin wire cutter to exactly cut any requested measure and at the same time wave away any flies that were circling around these masses of delicious delicacies.

At the end of each financial year, all books would be handed over to the store and each customer's dividend would be calculated. An official mass pay-out would then take place the following Saturday morning, in one of the local city halls. Ours was the Mason Hall in the High Street. Such events caused great excitement, and long, noisy queues formed, all anxiously awaiting their divi. This was desperately needed by most families whereby they could clear most of their debts, a godsend to the city.

One such dividend paid for the first holiday as a family together (my mother, father, and young Bill). This was to Coupar Angus, some seventeen miles north of Dundee. Money was in short supply, so they decided to book into a bed and breakfast. However, the arrangement was that they bought enough bacon and eggs to last all week, which being a young couple, they dutifully handed over to the landlady, Miss Burnett. She was almost bent double with rheumatics but made the family very welcome and took charge of the food. On the bus journey to Coupar Angus, a passenger forewarned them of Miss Burnett as having the reputation of being "fell grippy" and worth watching. This was born out to be true on the third morning of the holiday, when she informed my mother that the family had run out of bacon and eggs. In fact, she had been using the food to feed the other houseguests. Also, they had paid for fresh milk each morning, but on the second day, it was found to be sour. The old lady did not appear to understand or comprehend what was being said, but from then on, they decided to eat out. Other than that hiccup, the rest of the holiday was fine.

Ramsay MacDonald

Meanwhile, the political scene was becoming very confused, and the lives of working-class people were being played out against a continuing national background of extreme generic poverty. This was capped by the introduction of extensive means testing and the ultimate fall of the first Socialist government. It was led by Ramsay MacDonald. However, he did not fall with his party. Instead, he was persuaded to lead the first National Coalition government. A Socialist prime minister was leading a government that consisted solely of Conservative and Liberal MPs. To add to this imprudent dilemma, there was also a naval mutiny at Invergordon and widespread hunger marches, which culminated in the great Hunger March of 100,000 people (1932—1934), who finally descended on London. The prime minister refused to meet with the marchers' delegation, which only deepened the crises; by 1935, MacDonald, who was by then an ill man, resigned. He died in 1937, just prior to the start of the Second World War. Quoting Robert Burns, "The best-laid plans of mice and men gang afta-gley."

With the effect of the depression still being felt throughout the country and the introduction of means testing, along with continuing mass unemployment, my father, along with most of the shipyard workers, lost his job. And then, only two decades after the previous war, the threat of a second war with Germany was starting to loom over the horizon. As my father said, this was not a new war; it merely was a continuation of the last, which was ended by means of the armistice, not a surrender. It simply gave Germany a respite and a chance to rearm. I wonder if there was something, anything, that we could have learnt from this as I feel that it could only have been the intervening hand of the divine that prepared and readied us for the 1939 war. Only a miracle allowed us to prevail as the workers of this country, who were the ones again expected to do the fighting, were by no means ready for such a brutal conflict.

Duty Called

After the seizure of power in Germany by Hitler in 1933, and his cruelties explicitly towards the Jews and disabled, it was clear that a war was pending. This was despite the waving gesture of a piece of paper by current Prime Minister Neville Chamberlain. The truth was only too clear to the working class who knew what lay ahead of them. Once again, they were expected to put right what politicians could not. It may also seem strange, but by 1939, many were glad to see the onset of war; my father pointed out that everyone knew a war was coming, so at least, they would all get back to work. Both my parents were called up for National Service duty. Sandy, who was in his forties and had already served his country, was sent back on war work as an iron driller in the shipyard, which had suddenly become extremely busy. My mother, who had again started work in the dental surgery, was exempt from service as she had a young child at school, but as part of the war effort, she was recruited into the Red Cross. She attended classes in first aid, and her two prime targets for practice were Sandy and her young son, Bill. Often Bessie would have them bandaged like Egyptian mummies with tourniquets, arm and leg bandages, and head caps. Sandy was also recruited into the National Fire Brigade Service. This came with a uniform, which was a fair fit, but Bessie altered it until perfect; she wanted her man to at least look the part of a fireman.

This was not the case for many new recruits, as Bessie reminisced. Before she had met Sandy, Bessie and her friend Meg had watched a fire engine screech to a halt in Victoria Road. It was attending a chimney fire, which was a regular occurrence in tenement blocks. Soot would often build up in the chimney passage and if not swept out regularly, deposits would cause a blockage that could unexpectedly ignite. The chimney would then bellow and roar as air was sucked up through the chimney vent. This would often cause a blowback whereby soot fell into the hearth, spilling over onto the floor and carpets and filling the room with thick, black grime that covered everything and took weeks to clean.

As Meg and Bessie watched the big, handsome firemen jump down from the fire engine, there was a pause. Suddenly, as if from nowhere, a wee man appeared, much smaller than Sandy's five feet, two inches. Admittedly he was wearing a uniform, but it was meant for someone who was at least six feet tall. His hands had disappeared up the jacket sleeves, the trouser lengths trailed the ground, and his whole head just fell into the helmet and vanished. Then, and apparently full of business, he tried, by waving his arms about in a ridiculous fashion, to control the small assemblage of people who had gathered. Meg then recognised him and his antics. He was the husband of a friend.

At that point, the two women, who were susceptible to seeing the funny side of things, disintegrated into fits of laughter, so much so that they had to run away into a nearby alleyway (close) before he saw them. He of course thought that there was no one quite like him, and he was right. There, in the close, the two women, with tears rolling down their faces, almost laughed their heads off at what they had just seen. Both stood waving their arms about in imitation of this poor friend and holding onto each other for support. As Meg often recalled, "Ma een nearly fell oot ma heed when a saw him."[34] Bessie said later that it was one of the funniest "off the cuff" things she had ever seen, but it made her even more determined that her man's uniform would fit, and she did not mean fit for laughter.

---

[34] "My eyes almost fell out of my head when I saw him."

I Can Do It

Along with Bessie's part-time job, this had been just enough to sustain the family. But as if things could not get any worse, after six weeks of idleness, Sandy was "means tested," and the result was devastating. It meant that his unemployment benefit, which was a mere twenty-one shillings per week (£1.05), was cut to only half a crown (25p). The family was now in dire straits. My proud father was forced to return home, dejected, and humiliated with only half a crown in his hand—his only contribution to the household. He looked at his wife and with tears in his eyes tried to explain. "You see, wife, they've cut my money because you're earning, and this is what they gave me." She looked straight into his eyes and put her arms round him. "Things will get better, Sandy," she said optimistically. "You put that in your pocket. A man needs to carry some money." My father's pride and position as head of the household had been severely demised. He felt that in some way he was inadequate, unable to support his family, and using a common Dundee vernacular, he had become a "kettle boiler." My father's great fear was that he, as head of his family, would have to undergo the humiliating process of approaching the parish for help.

The decision was made that my mother would look for full-time work in the mills, which was no easy task as they too were in a depressed state. Bessie often recalled the days when she, along with more than a hundred similar women, anxiously stood outside factory doors waiting for news of possible work. One dismal, cold April morning, a rumour circulated that a few jobs were available at Prainy's jute mill in Henderson Wynd. A mass movement of women surged through the town centre, my mother among them, all intent on reaching the factory gates first. As the foreman appeared from behind the closed gates, the crowd suddenly surged forward. Some women, standing in the front ranks, were pushed to the ground, and trampled over. This orderly assemblage of womenfolk quickly turned into a squabbling mass as women were pushing each other in all directions with the inevitable exchange of harsh words. My mother, who had been in the front row, was steadily pushed back and lost her place. The foreman (or gaffer) who had seen these all too often bickering spats ignored it as the norm, and from behind the safety of the closed gates, he called out, "Are there any Boyd Patent Twisters here?" Bessie, who had not done that sort of work before, and through sheer temper at being pushed back, jumped higher than anyone else and shouted, "I am! I can do it!" The gaffer pointed straight at her and said, "You," and then at two other hopeful women, "You and you, in." Out of more than a hundred women, only three had been chosen, and Bessie was one of them. Although she had never heard of the term "Boyd Patent Twisting," from her experience in the mills, she knew that it would be easy to learn, so once again she was back in the mills. Her wage was £1.50 per week, and between that and Sandy's dole money, they were fine.

Each day, Sandy, with Bill in his arms, walked from factory to factory, foundry to foundry, and then on to the shipyard, prepared to do any kind of work. However, the whole country was experiencing the effect of this awful dilemma, but that was of little conciliation when the drama fell at one's own doorstep. Some families were hit much harder than others. In many cases, extreme poverty and malnutrition took place, which of course often led to disease and depression, and the occasional suicide. Most homes were infested with vermin; mice, rats, and bugs openly crawled up the walls while nourishing themselves on the flower-based paste that was used as adhesive for hanging cheap wallpaper, which covered cracked and broken plaster. Some households had their electricity and gas cut off due to non-payment of bills. This caused extreme hardship during the long, damp, and cold nights of winter. There developed a serious drink problem in the city, particularly among out-of-work men, which in turn often led to the breakup of family units.

Desperate efforts were made to try to help each other during these times of extreme hardship. Neighbours would look after each other's children, even feeding them and passing on hand-down clothes when needed, knowing full well that shortly they too may be in similar extreme distress. One elderly widow on Dallfield Walk accepted the children of a neighbour to live with her until the family got back on its feet. My grandmother, Mary, always had a large pot of hot soup ready for anyone who needed it, and there was always a steady stream of takers. Nevertheless, despite these desperate and frantic circumstances that the working society was going through, people always had time for each other; there was a bond among people that does not exist today.

There were only intermittent periods of work for Sandy during these long stretches of unemployment, and it was then that my brother was born, in 1931. When possible, during the occasional and sporadic periods when work was available, Sandy often returned to his trade as an iron driller in the shipyard or Blackness Foundry, but he would try any type of occupation and was grateful for anything that was offered. Often this meant employment in Watson's Dye Works at the bottom of Forebank, since converted into flats. He would work long hours with different dyes that were used as colourants for the finished jute fabric. It meant that he would return home each night stained in a multitude of colours. This caused my father's hands to become painfully infected by his old nemesis, dermatitis, which again caused much idle time. There was no welfare state that could step in and help those in difficulty, and if a family had no income, then they were extremely poor indeed. Families were often broken up, the siblings being spread out among the extended family of aunts and uncles, grandparents, and in extreme cases, even friends. These poor working-class people would do almost anything for a job.

Of those in work, the wages were low, and they were at the mercy of the whimsical moods of the boss or gaffers. A worker (man or woman) could be dismissed for the most minor of offences (sometimes none) to which there was no recourse. A few unscrupulous gaffers regularly took bribes (back handers), which sometimes only amounted to the offer of a pint down in the local pub each Friday. But occasionally this was not the case and a few unprincipled men in authority would accept inducements and favours for issues that were not so innocent. In this way, rights were frequently violated in more ways than one; things were not easy, and this applied especially to the younger women, and all for a job.

None of this applied to my folks, and my father, who was by no means a soft man, handed over his closed wage packet each Friday to his wife. They both realised that every penny was needed, and that the family was infinitely more important than nights in the pub. Like most of the womenfolk, Bessie was the purser in the family, but she always made sure that her man could afford to have a few pints at the weekend. These women somehow always managed to lay money aside for emergencies that would habitually appear from nowhere. New shoes for the family, school jotters, or the Sosh bill were often met from this emergency fund.

Modest Pride

Win these far off days, women rarely frequented pubs, which were the strict domains of men. Here, in male fashion, in their "local," they would put the world to right, and for most men, this was enough. The Ellenbank bar was my father's local, into which his wife had never entered. In fact, Bessie had never seen the inside of a pub, except on one occasion. This happened in their later years, when my folks had retired and were on holiday in Ireland; this was the only time Bessie could claim to have been abroad. The weather was good that summer, and one hot, sunny afternoon as they strolled through Dublin, Sandy fancied a beer, so he took his wife into a pub, telling her that it was an Irish hotel. There, he bought her a double Bailey's Irish Cream, after which she wouldn't stop talking, which was not unusual for Bessie, but even more so on this occasion. That was the only alcoholic drink he ever bought her, other than an occasional advocate.

Overall, my parents had a good and successful marriage. At the start of their married life, all appeared well, at least for the first year. Both had a job, and Bessie had methodically saved enough money to pay for their own wedding and semi-furnish their two-roomed but-n-ben home. They had even enough for luxury goods, which included a central carpet in the front room and waxcloth floor covering (the forerunner to linoleum or vinyl) around the edgings. This room, some ten feet by ten feet square, had an additional recess, which was wide enough to accommodate a double bed. It was like all other but-n-ben homes where the main living area acted as the kitchen, dining, and bedroom space. The scantly furnished back room was approximately the same size but without the recess. However, they had managed to floor it entirely with waxcloth; later it was furnished with a fashionable, ornate, double, dark-oak wardrobe with a full-length mirror between the doors, which gave the impression that the room contained more furniture than it did. This, as in many similar working-class family homes, gave the impression that even in such lowly and underprivileged conditions there existed an element of modest pride.

A large rope-driven window overlooked the back green, which contained a washhouse and a communal midden recess area that accommodated two entire tenement blocks, which consisted of some forty families. In the midden area, half a dozen heavy, galvanised bins were filled to the brim each week with household refuse. They often overflowed and spilled onto the surrounding ground, attracting all kinds of unwelcome creatures. Each Monday, the bins were emptied by the refuse collectors or binmen ("scaffies"), who carried these hefty objects over their shoulders, dumping the stinking contents into an open-sided cart. During this process, as much litter was dropped as was lifted and carried off. Cleaning up after these binmen was a weekly ritual among the wives and mothers who had organised a designated rota; they would clean the bin recess area as best they could, which within days would once again be filled with refuse to overflowing. My folks were luckier than some tenants as their flat was part of a tenement block that had just been upgraded to include inside toilets. This saved the indignity for all to see one having to walk along the open landing to the toilet, located on the stairwell, and which was communal to several residents. These less lucky tenants always had, somewhere in their small but-in-ben, an emergency commode, and that often was just a bucket.

A Woman's Place

Each Friday, Sandy (like most married men) would dutifully hand over to his wife his hard-earned wage packet, unopened, there being absolute trust between them. However, this was not always the case between some husbands and wives, and often the wife never knew what her husband earned. She would only receive what he thought she needed (or deserved) to run the house. The rest of his income was held back, going into his own pocket. It did not stay there for long, as often it was spent in the pub or just as stupidly lost to a bookie's runner while betting on the horses. There would be a bookie's runner on most street corners. They would act as the middlemen between the punter (the one placing the bet) and the bookmaker. The runner's main quality, apart from loyalty to the bookie, was his running speed. He had to be faster than the police; otherwise, all bets were off. In fact, the oversized well-fed members of the constabulary were no match for the surefooted swiftness of a runner, so they simply didn't bother in any chase. They mostly turned a blind eye to such an activity—and often themselves participating in it.

If the woman was also working, which was normally the case, then it was expected that her entire wage would be contributed to the household budget. Despite the wife's earnings often exceeding that of her husband, the women had very few rights. They neither had the right to vote nor rent their own home unless they had acquired the signature of a man (a father, brother, friend, or husband). This was a great handicap to a single woman, and for a degree of security, women were required to be married. But even then, life could be hazardous as silent domestic violence and ill treatment was commonplace. The wife was often totally at the mercy of the husband's unspoken cruelty; the law turned a blind eye and habitually ignored the wife's frantic and desperate cries for help. Of course, some cowardly men (and there were always some) took advantage of their wife's predicament, mistreating them at will, knowing that there would be little chance of any repercussions. In fact, such men would often arrogantly boast of their domestic offences to their equally depraved cronies in the local pub. No woman of any character would attempt to patronise these male-dominated venues; this would be to their ultimate scorn and shame. It was here, in the strict male domain, that one half of our species reinforced the habit that they had cultivated as youths and which they had so often seen in the privacy of their own homes— abuse of the wife. The pub was strictly a male drinking den and fuelled many of the problems that were rife in the city.

Neither were the police immune to such acts of cruelty. I remember, as a young boy, overhearing a police officer explain to a colleague how he had "slapped [his] wife around" the previous night, just to keep her in her place. Both men laughed and sniggered at this; I was young at the time and could not even imagine my father striking my mother. But there it was, two officers of the law condoning such violence as if it were the norm.

It took a long time before my trust or respect for any advocate of the law returned. This was certainly not a good time for women.

Poor Meg

Meg Morrison was one such deprived woman, and things certainly did not work out so well for Bessie's best friend. Despite having helped my mother choose the right man for a husband, she did not do the same for herself. Bessie knew from the start that her friend had made a bad choice and that he was not the right one for her, if for anybody. How can things be so obvious to others but not to oneself? Hints were dropped as to the type of person he was, inferences made about his character, even suggestions as to how to untangle herself from his grasp were made, but to no avail. She was a typical Dundee strong-minded woman and was convinced that he was the right man to marry.

It was not long after the wedding that she realised the extent of her folly, but it was too late. For a woman in those days, there was little recourse. They simply had to live with the consequences, and the consequences for Meg were bad. Meg died at the early age of 26, just after the birth of her child, named Margaret, after her mother. Bessie was godmother. The child went to live with her maternal grandparents, whereby all contact was lost with the father.

The husband of Meg had the audacity to walk behind his wife's coffin in the funeral cortege, with his head bowed in grief. As he passed by, contempt was displayed by the onlookers who lined the streets. Men booed him, and women turned their backs. I wonder what went through his mind. If anything, it certainly was not remorse or regret for his actions. There was not only sadness in the air that day but also great malice for this unworthy husband. As men and women alike displayed their abhorrence and repugnance at his very presence, the only safeguard he had was from a priest. Throughout his own wife's funeral procession, this husband found it necessary to seek security by walking alongside this reluctant priest. How could men like that live with such memories imprinted on their mind?

He was never arrested, charged, or cautioned by the police. There was no legal chastisement of any kind; the authorities rarely involved themselves in the internal affairs of a family. The all-male police force, and legal system, had little regard for women's rights and domestic violence. I suppose, in an environment such as this, my mother could have been regarded as lucky, although I very much doubt if she would have put up with such nonsense. In that respect, my father was a placid, good-natured man. Neither he nor my mother had ever seen violence towards the mother of their respective families, so such a trait was simply not in their nature.

It took a long time before Bessie recovered from her best friend's unnecessary and premature death. She could think of nothing else for months; memories flooded back of the days at the dancing and dance classes where they partnered each other so often. This event marked the end of Bessie's young, carefree days, and although she had experienced hardship and pain herself, it was this episode in her life that changed her into a more serious and mature person.

As she gradually recovered from the loss of Meg, Bessie started to look to the future and prepare for life with Sandy. They were lucky in that they both had jobs while courting and were able to save. However, despite having little spare money to spend, life during this frugal courtship was not taken all too seriously. They were still outgoing and still enjoyed themselves, but they knew that the time had come for their wilder dancing days to end.

They spent more time in the company of each other's family; Bessie was well liked by her prospective father-in-law, who often favoured her opinion over his own sons, including Sandy. She also developed a tight bond with the mother-in-law, which was to the utter dismay of the other wives.

CHAPTER 12

The Second War

War Preparations

Although Sandy may have looked the part of a fireman, his ability as a firefighter was somewhat in doubt, as was the rest of his squad. After each fire practice, he would return home to a family who anxiously awaited to hear the next episode in the saga of Sandy the fireman. Between not finding the fire hydrants, losing hoses, and even once his squad lost the fire engine, the family was entertained all evening. My father often said that if Dundee had ever been blitzed, or seriously bombed, it would not have stood a chance. "It wid jist hay ti burnt doon."[35]

One of his memorable stories occurred while returning from fire practice. An extremely excited woman stopped him in Alexander Street and, thinking that he was the beat policeman, wanted him to sort out a domestic problem that had apparently got out of hand. Now despite his uniform, few people would have mistaken my father as a policeman. But when attempting to explain that he was not part of the police force, she would not accept it. "What are yi dressed up like a bobby, are yi dafty?"[36] she shouted at him. He told her he was

---

[35] "It would just have burnt down."

[36] "Why are you dressed like a policeman, are you daft?"

a fireman. "Weel you'll jist hay ti day"[37] was her retort as he was dragged off to settle a family dispute in his capacity as a part-time fireman. There was always something funny that happened during these nights on duty. "What happened tonight, Dad?" would be the first question by young Billy as his father entered the house. Sandy would sit down, take his boots and jacket off, and then start in his storytelling manner the events of that evening. While this was going on, Billy would of course dress up in his dad's uniform.

He was a very entertaining man when telling a story, and no matter how often he repeated the same tale, it was always just as amusing. Often, he was asked to tell certain stories again.

One favourite tale involved a Saturday fair in Dudhope Park (sometimes referred to as the Barrack Park as Barrack Road led into the grounds). Here, the main attraction was a series of demonstrations by the city fire service. They demonstrated to the public how efficient their local fire service was and how quickly they could respond to an emergency. One particularly important exhibit involved my father's team. They were to display how competent the fire service was at extinguishing a blaze. Once the hose was attached to the hydrant, this squad of adeptly organised men lined up together and held the nozzle of the hose towards the fire. Nothing happened. Someone had forgotten to turn the water on. No matter as a member of another team did the honours. Unfortunately, this proficiently organised team had laid the hose down and it was now resting on the ground. A surge of cold water gushed from the nozzle of this now unmanned hose, which caused it to rise some twenty feet into the air, drenching everybody in range. It then reeled and twisted like a snake along the ground, knocking some women off their feet and causing them to surf along the wet grass under the pressure. No one seemed to be in control as the wriggling hosepipe showered all around, and this included a policeman who was knocked clean off his bicycle. A fortune teller's tent was lifted out of its securing pegs, revealing a surprised and soaked old lady who had earlier predicted it would rain,

---

[37] "Well! You will just have to do."

but not quite as heavy as in this pantomime. It was pandemonium. The crowd scattered in all directions; other fire teams could only look on in amazement as the bedlam unfolded. My father's squad tried to catch hold of the hose end, but they were helplessly carried along with the force of the water.

Eventually, someone took the initiative and managed to struggle through the blinding spray from the reeling lurches of the hose and switched the water off. Things immediately settled, and it became clear that an area within a radius of fifty yards from the hose was a drenched wipe-out zone with overturned stalls, prams, and benches. But no one had injuries that were worthy of mention, and as it was a warm Saturday afternoon, the saturated onlookers, in typical Dundee fashion, who had more to contend with in their lives than a drop of water, quickly dried off.

As things got back to normal, the fair continued as if nothing untoward had happened. Unfortunately, the fortune teller was correct, and the whole afternoon's outing was cut short due to a sudden downpour.

That same Saturday evening, as the fire team drove back to their station in Dudhope Park, and as it was an hour before the pubs closed, at half past nine, they unanimously decided to drop into Cookie's bar on the Hilltown. However, this drop-in venue for a "quick" pint was not a good idea. The week before, two of the squad had been forcibly evicted from the same public house. The men had been on practice duty, at the end of which a trivial but heated dispute developed with their driver. The driver then deliberately left them behind to walk back to the depot, carrying the hose. Cookie's bar lay on route so not surprisingly the two men dropped in for refreshments. Rather than carry the hose into the pub, they abandoned it outside at the door entrance before stepping in.

However, things were slightly different for the next customer. Some men often fall out of such establishments, but few would normally fall in; however, this one did. With a fish supper tucked under his arm, the customer fell forward into the pub and cracked his head on the edge of the bar, over which slid his fish supper. He then fell straight into the arms of Mick, the local heavyweight bruiser, who unfortunately happened to be standing at the bar, in the wrong place at the wrong time. He fell backwards to the ground, bumping his head on the way. The original bleeding customer by this time was now out cold, so one of the firemen bent over and opened the paper bag. "He'll no be need'in this then," he said, tucking into the chips.

However, Mick, was not out cold, and as he lifted himself off the ground and rose to his feet, he growled at the rest of the drinking customers. He was not a happy man. "Wha put that hose doon at the door?"[38] There then followed a few exchanges of nasty verbosities, after which a melee of bodies, arms, and legs were scattered over the sawdust-covered floor. The proprietor, more for their safety, decided to unceremoniously eject the two firemen from his establishment, along with the remnants of the fish supper.

It was against this rather tarnished reputation that the firemen trooped in, all in full uniform, including helmets. The bruiser, Mick, was standing in his usual place at the bar as once again the two firemen came face to face with their nemesis, but all was well. They shook the oversized hand of this big man, and each bought him a pint.

Dundee people quickly forgive past demeanours—a trait that still exists today. However, by this time, gossip had spread throughout the area that a fire engine was parked outside Cookie's pub. Rumours then escalated, suggesting that the pub was on fire, then it was ablaze, and finally as the tittle-tattle continued, it transpired that Cookie's had burnt to the ground. This was a local disaster of the first order, so by the time the firemen had finished their drinks and appeared from within, they were met by almost the entire male population of the Hilltown. On realising that it was only to water themselves and not the pub, the assembled mass let out an almighty roar of relief, bonnets were thrown into the air, and the firemen were treated like firefighting heroes.

It was said that Cookie's did more business that Saturday night than it did for the rest of the week. As far as the firefighters were

---

[38] "Who put that hose down at the door?"

concerned, far from an unceremonious ejection, they were thereafter warmly welcomed.

A Nazis Spy

Jessie Jordan, born in Glasgow (1887), married a German national and became a citizen of her adopted country. Jordan was her first husband, but he was killed in the 1914–18 war. She later married her brother-in-law, but that marriage ended in divorce, after which she returned to Scotland—to Dundee, where she set up a hairdressing shop in Kinloch Street. During her time in Germany, she had been recruited by the Abwehr[39] to spy for the Nazis, which she did, and for two years she was the hub of a spy ring that stretched from the United States back to Hamburg. Fortunately, she was not the best of spies and was discovered before the war started, so no real damage was done. Jordan was found guilty and incarcerated for four years. On her release in 1941, she was rearrested and interned for the remainder of the war. After that, she was deported back to Hamburg, dying there in 1954.

This woman admitted that she became a spy simply for the excitement. But that was not the case for other more devious traitors who tried to overthrow none other but the British government. The anti-Semite Archibald Maule Ramsay and his wife, Lady Ninian Crichton Stuart, created the Right Club in 1939 for this purpose. It was made up of right-wing sympathisers from the aristocracy, many of whom had great influence in government circles.

Jessie Jordan was a spy and was lucky not to have been hanged, but she was not in the same league as the Ramsays. Ramsay was caught but never prosecuted, although he was interned during the war years. Strangely enough, he kept his parliamentary seat and salary until the 1945 Labour general election landslide, dying in 1955. What does this tell you about the aristocracy of that day?

---

[39] Germany's espionage service.

The Phony War

War had been declared against Germany, but the conflict had not yet arrived at our doorstep. This period was known as the "Phony War." Nevertheless, life had become increasingly hectic. Our ally, Poland, had been invaded, followed by the fall of France. The British Expeditionary Force along with the remnants of the French army had been miraculously plucked from the shores of Dunkirk (over 300,000 men). Hundreds of privately owned vessels were involved in the rescue, which included one of the Dundee to Newport ferry boats.

When the Phony War was over, frantic preparations were underway throughout the land to repel any threat of an invasion; the most poignant icons were the ominous appearance of the air-raid shelters and pillboxes. These shelters, built of brick and reinforced concrete, were designed to withstand the collapse of a bombed tenement building and vulnerable only to a direct hit. The civilian occupants of these shelters were at the mercy of the events that were taking place outside, and the success of our armed forces. Also, of course, my father's firefighting service.

The shelters normally had two entrances at diagonally opposite corners. Inside were several rooms with hard, wooden benches along the walls. There was no form of heating, and only candles could be used for lighting, which gave a menacing sensation as everyone sat together. Everyone had their own space in the shelter, which made it easy to see if anyone was missing; the seats were taken up by the elderly and mothers with young children. During the day, women formed a rota to sweep out and clean the rooms of these shelters. However, the warning wail of the sirens, which could occur at any time of the day, indicated that an air raid was imminent; all tenants immediately collected their children and belongings and descended into the cold, dark sanctuary of the shelter. This mostly occurred at night, particularly when the moon was bright, thus allowing the German bombers to see the coastline and find landmarks; they would also follow river systems, such as the Tay, to their pre-planned destinations.

In the cold environment of the dark shelters, blankets would be shared along with hot water bottles, and occasionally a crumpled paper bag containing hard-boiled sweeties, "boilings," would be passed from one tired and weary neighbour to another. These sweets would either be crunched by those who had their own teeth or sucked by those who didn't, making a low, odd cracking munch among the tenants as they sat momentarily motionless in this moment of crisis. Slowly conversations would start up between those sitting close by. As conversations gradually spread throughout this confined space, the volume, not to mention the humidity, correspondingly rose. This was the period of catch-up on the daily gossip, and as the volume got louder, to make oneself heard, one had to shout, and shout loudly. It felt as if the very walls were vibrating from the human voices.

After a while, as if by magic the noise would subside as quickly as it had started. This would be the time for entertainment, started by a lone singer. Soon the small, close community would join in until the entire group was singing. An old-fashioned sing-along followed, whereby all the songs from the current musicals, war songs, and songs from yesteryear were sung. Then, almost like clockwork, the storytelling session followed, when the older men would tell of earlier campaigns, as far back as the Boer Wars by some. There were always joke-tellers in the company. (Some Dundee women could be coarse.) Some of the stories would be close to the knuckle, but all ended in hoots of laughter. This continued until the all-clear siren sounded, when all would collect their belongings and return to the "safety" of their homes.

Sandy went on duty at the sound of the first siren, and Bessie sat with the rest of the neighbours, her first aid box at hand and Bill at her side. However, come August 1943, there was a new arrival in the shelter, a ten-and-a-half-pound baby. I was duly deposited into a small baby gasbag and placed on my mother's lap on top of her first aid box. During these nightly evacuations, I would sit with the rest of the company, waiting for the all-clear siren, my first steps being taken in the air-raid shelter.

Of course, I remember nothing of these experiences but was told that I remained wide-awake to all that was going on. I, like the rest of those huddled together, was at the mercy of others, and all were wishing that the nightmare would stop.

Party Politics

Dundee would appear to have been vulnerable to blitzing at the hands of German bombers, but that never took place, although the threat was always there. My father said that Lord Haw-Haw (the American William Brooke Joyce) had said in one of his frequent German propaganda broadcasts, which had become extremely popular and a source of entertainment to the British, that the city would never be deliberately bombed as it was the only part of Britain to have the good sense to throw Winston Churchill out; he was removed as the city's incumbent MP in the 1922 general election.

During this early period of the twentieth century, Dundee politics had little to do with "King Jute." Churchill had held Dundee as his parliamentary seat (for the Liberals) from 1908. However, this, the ultimate embarrassment of an electoral defeat, was made even worse as it was inflicted by the Prohibitionist candidate Edwin Scrymgeour, the only member of the Prohibition Party ever to be elected to the Westminster Parliament. Women had a great deal to do with this defeat. They had just won their democratic right to vote in the 1922 General Election; by the way, the city was never bombed by intent. This was not to the liking of Churchill, who doggedly opposed the suffragette movement. So this Liberal defeat had little to do with the Prohibitionist movement, whose main theme and strategy was to prevent the spread of demon drink that was particularly prevalent among the working-class of the day. It was a protest vote particularly due to Churchill's unpopularity among women. Edwin Scrymgeour held the city until 1931, when he was succeeded by Florence Horsburgh. She became the first woman cabinet minister to serve in a Conservative government and the first female privy councillor.

Edwin Scrymgeour had been a well-known and a well-liked figure for a long time in Dundee, and his electoral victory in his own hometown encouraged the Dundee people to give the vanquished Churchill a rousing farewell. Among the melee at the rail station was my father, accompanied by my mother, who was there simply to make sure my father avoided trouble. He said that during Churchill's final and heavily heckled address to the crowd, he allegedly remarked that he would see the grass grow over the Dundee mills, and he did. He never forgave the Dundonians, but neither did they forgive nor forget that unguarded remark. I remember, as a small boy, the boos, jeers, and foot stamping from any picture house audience in the city each time this man's face appeared on the screen.

Despite electing a Prohibitionist, Dundee was by no means a dry city, but the very act of electing such a person described the mocking extent of disdain felt towards Churchill. Although Lord Haw-Haw was a figure of comic derision, here he had certainly touched a raw nerve that rang true among the crumbling tenement blocks of this ancient burgh. For this humiliating defeat, Churchill never forgave the Dundonians. He had been their MP for fourteen years, after which he never once returned to the city. This was no loss, and he was little missed by the people of Dundee; it was simply his constituency, to which he rarely visited and contributed little. Neither forgive nor forget; it was remarkable that a man could rise so high in the eyes of some yet was regarded as having sunk so low in the eyes of others.

It took a world war before Dundee was rejuvenated, and even then, it was only a short-term respite.

A Day in Parliament

My father was certainly no supporter of the Prohibitionist Party, regarding its members as cranks who were totally unable to organise anything that involved more than two people. To prove his point, he always quoted in parrot-like fashion the time when Bessie and he joined an open-day Prohibitionist trip to London. It had been organised by Ned Scrimgeour himself and involved a visit to the seat of government at Westminster. Sandy sat in the speaker's chair, which greatly impressed my mother, who was overawed by the entire experience; she had never been so far away from home.

The whole trip was hailed a success, marred only at the end when boarding the bus in preparation for the long journey home. A headcount revealed that none other than a party official was missing. After a lengthy delay, the police were informed, and only then could the exhausted party set off.

It was not until the next day when newspaper headlines revealed that a certain high official in the Dundee division of the Scottish Prohibitionist Party had been arrested. He had been charged in London for drunk and disorderly behaviour and causing an affray. Some advert for the veto-endorsing party that totally rejected the consumption of alcohol. As my father often jokingly remarked, "Some are fine, but some are just a bunch o' hypocrites, oot fur what they can get."

The War and Its Consequences

When the war did come, it was long and hard and was the most terrible of conflicts. Many of Dundee's young men and women were sacrificed as they played their part in the defeat of Hitler and the Nazis. But the city, as Lord Haw-Haw predicted, was never threatened. The city would have been vulnerable to firebombing due to the highly inflammable nature of jute. It was also a ship and submarine repair base, and with the rail bridge stretching some two and a half miles across the Tay estuary, one would imagine it to be an early prime target for an enemy blitz, but it never came. Only a handful of bombs ever fell on the city during this horrendous conflict, and that was probably because of enemy aircraft ridding themselves of any remaining bombs before returning home. The city continued to supply the war effort through its shipyards, foundries, and ammunition factories. The jute mills produced millions of essential sandbags, which were critical to the armed forces and public. Nevertheless, the fear that it would soon be Dundee's turn to suffer like so many other cities (on both sides of the conflict) was always there.

The Luftwaffe bombers, with their eerie drone, easily distinguishable from our own, continually flew over the city; it was this whining bleat of hundreds of enemy aircraft on 13 March 1941 that caused the residents of Alexander Street to filter with uncommon haste into the shelters, all fearing that their time had come. All except my father, who was off duty that night and was snuggly tucked up in bed, sound asleep. This was his first night off for some time, and after a full day's work, he was exhausted. My mother could not get him to believe that there were droves of bombers flying overhead and that they may all be killed at any moment. "Yir dreamin, wuman. Come back ti bed"[40] was his reaction as he point-blankly refused to get up.

In the morning, he was shocked to hear that Clydebank, on the west coast, had been blitzed.

The second night of this blitz was different; all were up at the sound of the sirens. Sandy was on fire duty that night and was in the process of putting on his uniform, in his own methodical way. The family had to wait as he meticulously tied his shoelaces while a large proportion the Luftwaffe air force few overhead. "For God's sake, hurry up, Dad, or we'll a be killed!" my mother shouted, but Dad did not hurry. The reason he gave was ludicrous; he explained that if he hurried, he might trip over his shoelaces, fall down the stairs, and break his neck.

When Bessie eventually got into the shelter and sat down, placing Bill firmly on her knee, she, with great annoyed frustration, told the rest of the tenants what had happened. They, looking for some light relief in the cold darkness of the shelter, erupted into laughter. It was only then that Bessie saw the funny side of the situation and joined in. After that, the neighbours would often jokingly rib my father, asking if his shoelaces were tied.

---

40   "You're dreaming, woman. Come back to bed."

After only two decades of relative peace, the world had once again plunged itself into the wasteful preoccupation of war; the reward was to suffer its aftermath for years to come and the loss of an entire European generation.

It affected everyone, some far more than others, as was discovered when the many concentration camps throughout Europe were opened for all to see. It was discovered that 6 million Jewish lives had been pointlessly wasted, all in the name of Nazi ideology. The atrophic living skeletons who survived were only the tip of the iceberg, and the death toll could have been as high as 17 million, including slaves, the Romani society, and many of the mentally and physically disabled. All were systematically robbed of everything they had (to feed the Nazi war machine), then tortured, and finally murdered. Many of the dead were then further defiled by shattering their jawbones and removing gold fillings from their teeth; some bodies were flayed, and their skin used in the making of such items as lampshades. These barbaric atrocities are unfit to be part of humankind's history, but it is all too true.

Like all wars, World War II has had a lot to answer for in terms of both soldiers and civilians, men and woman, young and old—all lost. It left behind bereaved families, ruined futures where ambitions were abandoned forever, and promising relationships broken. Almost everyone was affected. Some had more traumatic experiences than others, but each individual person and family had their own unique memories that stayed with them long after the war.

My cousin Jean (my uncle Jim's daughter, on my father's side) was a young girl of 16 at the start of the war. She worked in her aunt's sweet shop (Mrs Hunter) located at the foot of the Hilltown. Jean was an attractive girl and had several admirers, but there was one who was special and meant a lot to her. He was an American soldier who, while on army leave, tried to piece together his family roots from Scotland. They met in the shop while he purchased sweets and were immediately attracted to each other; she quickly learnt that he was based close by in Fife, so they started to meet regularly.

Over the weeks that followed, the relationship became quite close, and although still fleeting, romance was certainly in the air. Together they managed to find his grandmother and a few of his relatives who still lived in Dundee. The encounter was brief, but long enough for them to speak of a possible life together after the war. However, before plans were made, he was shipped off to fight. Contact was lost between the couple, and it was only through his new-found relatives that Jean discovered he had been fatally wounded, dying on a far-off beach in Normandy. Jean was devastated and retreated into herself for a long time. However, she was young and resilient, and like so many wartime couples, she was not alone. It was necessary to recover quickly from the depths of depression and restart, hopefully with new dreams and aspirations.

By this time, it was total war against Germany and its allies. Everyone lived from day to day not knowing what the outcome would be. Death may have come from the sky at any time, so people quickly forgot what happened yesterday; most lived only for the moment.

It was with this as a social backdrop that Jean met her second love. He was an officer in the Royal Air Force, and their romance stretched over several summer months. They were to be engaged, but he too was lost to the war, killed when his plane was shot down during a bombing raid over Germany. The shock of a second loss shattered Jean into a state of utter distress, from which she took months to recover. Support and sympathy poured out from the family, and that included her father, Jim. Unfortunately, Jim was not the most tactful of men and never seemed to catch the mood of any situation. In his usual unintended inimical way, his advice to his daughter was simple. "Diny meet any mare sodgers. They ah manage tae feenish up daid.[41]" Hardly fatherly comfort to a distraught daughter, but that was Jim.

---

[41] "Don't meet any more soldiers. They always manage to finish up dead."

Maria from Greece

As World War II came to an end, there was a great feeling of relief and hope for the future. However, things got off to a slow start. Idleness was back, so things seemed to be getting back to pre-war normality.

Bessie managed to get a part-time job as a shop assistant in Brown's tobacconist at the bottom of the Hilltown. So at least there was some money coming into the household. While there, she befriended many of the customers, often becoming confidante to their troubles, but one regular customer stood out. She was a Greek girl, called Maria, who came in each day for the daily newspaper, *The Telegraph*.

She met her Dundee husband while he was serving in Greece, where they married at the end of the war. This young girl thought that life would be so much better in Scotland. What a shock it must have been on discovering the fate that awaited her. My mother was the only one she trusted. To her, she professed her unhappiness and the regular ill treatment she received at the hands of her husband. Often, she would show my mother photographs of her family in Greece, including the day she got married. Maria was a beautiful, young bride with a long veil and tiara; her innocent face was full of hope and expectations for the future.

In the short while that she had been here, Maria had aged considerably. Now with a young son, the sparkle seen in the photographs had gone, replaced with apathy and fear. She would always appear just before six o'clock, as the shop was being closed for the evening, to collect the late afternoon newspaper and have a chat. Bessie always had one *Evening Telegraph* (the *"Telly"*) laid aside for Maria, but on this specific night, she was nowhere to be seen. Bessie waited for her, but there was no sign.

My mother thought that perhaps the baby was ill, so she decided to deliver the paper herself. Maria lived in the old maze of slum buildings at the bottom of the Hilltown, the same place where Bessie had gotten lost years before, but it had since become even more derelict. When she eventually found the front door, there was no letterbox; it had been sealed up. Bessie hesitated to knock as she felt that Maria would be embarrassed at her obvious poor living conditions. However, the *Telly* was important to people, so she lightly knocked.

The door opened very hesitantly, and Maria appeared. She was surprised but pleased to see her friend. "Your *Telly*, Maria," said my mother, handing it to her. Maria was so glad to see the paper, but she was trembling and in obvious distress. She beckoned my mother in. The only form of light came from two candles standing on the table, and in the faint glow, Bessie could just make out the shabby conditions this young woman was living in. As her eyes got used to the dimness, she then saw the marks on her arms. "Maria!" my mother exclaimed. "You're all bruised." Unmistakably, she had been beaten. Maria, pointing to the table and in a quivering voice, said, "He likes his paper to be there at night, but I didn't have time before he came home." Bessie felt her blood boil with rage. This was something that she could not tolerate; a Dundee man deliberately bringing his bride – *to this!*

At that instant, and it could not have been timed any better, the husband made his appearance at the front door. He immediately recognised Bessie from the corner shop and knew that she was related to the Pullars of the Hilltown; in addition, he had crossed swords with John McElroy, her brother, and he certainly didn't wish to repeat that encounter again by antagonising the older sister.

Bessie stared into the face of the husband, but for the sake of Maria, she held her temper back. "You lave her alain,"[42] she said in a disparaging but threatening voice. This threat to the husband was all too clear, as he stood saying nothing. Then, turning to Maria, she said, "I'll see you the morn, in the shop, ti mak share you're a right."[43] Maria nodded, and half smiled as Bessie pushed past this heavy lump that was blocking the doorway.

---

[42] "You leave her alone."
[43] "I'll see you tomorrow in the shop, to make sure you're all right."

Next day, as the shop was closing, Maria came in as usual. Her *Telly* was there on the counter, but before she left, Bessie closed the front door. "Maria," she said taking her hand and leading her to two chairs behind the counter. Bessie advised her to write home to her family, but she was too proud and would not let them know what she had come to. My mother then took Maria's hand. "Well," she said, looking at this poor, frightened girl. "I've got a suggestion, but only if it's fine with you. My man, Sandy, is now a member of the Ancient Order of Shepherds, and if you like, he can get you a house, and we can get a friend to sign it over to you." Maria's dulled eyes immediately lit up at the thought of freeing herself from the monster she was married to. "Oh, please, please," she said in her broken English, her eyes now sparkling. She started to gush with tears. Bessie told her to wait a few weeks and say nothing to anyone. Maria later said that these two weeks were the longest of her life, but as good as his word, Sandy found her a house close to one of his brothers, in Stirling Street.

For a while, Maria became one of the thousands of faceless millworkers, but she was free, leaving behind an abusive relationship and starting anew.

In time, Bessie left the tobacconist shop and the two women lost contact. It was at least a year later when in town one cold Saturday afternoon, they once again met. Despite the cold, they stood and reminisced for more than an hour. Maria explained that her husband had become an alcoholic and that her parents were helping her obtain a divorce. Her young son had been placed into a nursery and she was currently working in the Caldrum Street washy (laundrette). She also explained to Bessie that she was seriously thinking on returning home to Greece; Maria loved Dundee and its people, but her heart was still Greek. This may have been the best course of action for Maria and her son, who was young enough to make the switch without too much destress. She recognised that none of this would have been possible if it had not been for my mother urging her to make a change. She was so grateful that both women broke down and openly cried in the street. In the best continental style, she kissed Bessie on both cheeks, hugged her, and thanked her for restarting her life. The two women then parted, knowing that they may never meet again.

In fact, that was the last time they saw each other; Maria and her son left for home, and contact was lost.

CHAPTER 13

Then There Was Me

Another Sandy (I Think)

On 31 August 1943, a baby boy was born into the family, me. Born at home, I weighed in at ten and a half pounds and was named after my father, Alexander. The family was now complete, but I don't think this completeness was precision planned. My mother was in her fortieth year (old then for childbirth), and my father almost five years older, so let's say that I was a pleasant surprise. It was fondly pointed from both sides of the family that a late child would be a blessing to his parents; well, I hope I was.

Bessie, fearing that I would assume the same nickname as my father, Eck, decided to call me Allan, which had nothing to do with my true family name. Strangely enough, she was the only person ever to call my father by that nickname, but he was an easy-going man and went along with his wife's decision, just to please her. Allan stuck with me until my teenage years, when I assumed the title of Sandy (again short for Alexander), like my father. However, the older family members and friends continued to call me by the name they had always used; in fact, my uncle Jim (my mother's brother) wondered who Alexander was when he received his wedding invitation for my marriage. He genuinely thought that my name was Allan.

This nominal appellation caused a great deal of confusion in my early years. It had no bearing on anything and often caused muddled embarrassment and misunderstanding, including the school roll and the doctor's panel, but my mother was insistent. However, once I had started my secondary education, at Stobswell Boys' Junior Secondary School in Dundee, the pseudonym of Allan was shed, for good. All the old family members who knew me by this alias have now sadly gone, along with the name, Allan.

1945

Nevertheless, things were changing for the better in Dundee. And although my father had been paid off just after the war had finished, there was a feeling of positive confidence. People had all helped and stood by each other during this conflict, they had all been in the same boat at the same time for so long, and at last they could now see light at the end of a turbulent tunnel. There was now optimism and hope.

The family was unscathed, unlike the First World War, when my father lost three brothers. But now things were different. Due to the 1945 general election, a new post-war Labour government under Clement Attlee stormed into power with a majority of 145. The people of Dundee had played their part in this victory, and during that night of the election, as the result of each constituency was announced, dancing broke out in the city streets at the realisation of what had been done.

Despite the ruined state of the country, this Labour government introduced the NHS (National Health Service) and many other social benefits overseen by the Minister for Health, Aneurin (Nye) Bevan, admittedly with the help of America's 1948 Marshall Plan. This was a revelation, particularly to the working classes, as it allowed free medical care for all. Unfortunately, it was abused by some, who thought that the service was specifically for them, obtaining numerous pairs of spectacles and multiple sets of false teeth. People are strange.

It was also a time when my father thought, and I emphasise the word *thought,* that he was a communist, which in those days was a fashionable thing to be, especially among the working class. He of course never was, although he was an ardent trade unionist. He once mentioned to Bessie that a communist official called Willie Gallacher, from the local branch of the party, was due to make an open-air political speech the following Saturday afternoon, in Alexander Street's back green. Naturally, his wife, not knowing fully what a communist was, was the ideal person to tell, as she innocently spread the word around.

Well known as a public speaker, Gallacher was an outspoken radical and had become a local personality. Come noon that Saturday, most of the neighbours and some from the surrounding tenements lined themselves along the rows of terraced platies, making the whole area resemble an auditorium.

The speaker, to great applause from an expectant and enthusiastic audience, made his entrance from the rear end of a tenement close and, along with a few accompanying party officials, started to prepare the loudspeakers and microphone. With a certain amount of calculated pomp, an attached cable was passed through one of the windows on the bottom landing; the audience went silent as Gallacher, with solemn dignity and the microphone held in both hands as if about to pray, took centre stage. The audience waited and waited. The expectancy and anticipation of this now substantial crowd was at fever pitch. An official, thinking that there was a loose connection, hesitantly tapped one of the loudspeakers. Just at that instant, an exploding volume of noise blasted from both speakers, knocking the official back, but the din was not from Willie Gallacher. Instead, it was from Jimmy Shand and his Scottish Country Dance Band. The immediate response of the onlookers was to clap and "hooch." As the cable ran into a private tenant's flat, the music could not be switched off, and the tenant's preference was Jimmy Shand, not Willie Gallacher. The audience, who were expecting a serious political speech on behalf of the Communist Party, poured onto the green and immediately started to set up dance formations. Try though they may, the officials could do nothing but accept the situation and give Gallacher his due; he joined in. A full-scale party then erupted that went on for ages.

He was invited to return the next Saturday but politely declined, probably too busy entertaining. That was the end of my father's association with the Communist Party.

The Back Green

These back greens were not only places for speech-making. By the end of the war, most back greens were derelict, rundown areas filled with grim, obsolete, but solidly built air-raid shelters, a poignant reminder of more violent times, and all hidden behind the frontage of the grey Dundee tenements. Most of the available space that was left was nothing more than stone-littered, sandy wasteland dotted with broken-down walls and roofless washhouses.

The shelters had become sanctuaries for vermin, such as mice and rats. But once cleaned out, they were used as storage units for gardening equipment, bicycles, and the long, wooden tables and bench seats that were periodically set up and used by the neighbourhood for the children's outdoor parties. They were also areas of attraction not only for the younger children but also the older ones who, against the shelter walls, would often paint goalposts. Endless games of football would then ensue, often with no more than a tin can for a ball. In the limited space, the football pitch was not of the normally conventional shape. Opposite goals were frequently situated around a corner and on the wall of another shelter. Each opposing team could consist of two (including the goalkeeper) to twenty-two plus players, all enthusiastically wanting to kick the can.

The shelters were ideal for many other games, including hide-and-seek, kick the can, and hoppy-christy, along with countless others. But it was on the shelters that the most daring and even dangerous games took place. One's ability to jump from one shelter to another often set one's position in the pecking order among a group of boys.

Reputations could be won (or lost) on one jump. The harder jumps even had names: the twins (two jumps that had to be performed, one directly after the other), the dike (where the participant had to jump from one shelter roof on to a wall and in one continuous step leap onto the adjacent shelter), then of course the dreaded suicide (an enormous span between two shelters). I had the reputation of being a good jumper, but I never tried the suicide jump. If one missed, then one landed in the open bin (or midden) area below.

Periodically the police would appear, with notebook in hand, to take the name of anyone slow enough to be caught. Their appearance caused a mass evacuation from the shelters, out through the many tenement closes, or hiding inside the shelters themselves, which had many connecting rooms and two exit doors. I suppose the police appeared not so much to stop us playing on the shelters but more to stop stupid behaviour, as I have seen many accidents involving these jumps, some involving broken limbs. But it was all good fun and part of growing up in those post-war days. Also, one was always aware of the prestige involved among peers when a hard jump was successfully achieved.

Such activities went on in what was almost a closed, secret society among the youths of the day, and any jumping accomplishment that would attain a higher position in the group's pecking order was something that all parents were totally oblivious of.

In general, life once again had become worth living; it was there to be enjoyed, and fun and laughter were again genuine. We had done it, the war was over, and we had won. Despite the slump and unemployment, the future was looking good. Street (or back green) parties were held throughout the city, a tradition that continued long after the war had ended. The most convenient time to have such an activity was at the end of the long, school, summer holidays (the seven weeks) when the schoolkids were about to return to their neglected lessons; this return was all to the great relief of the mothers and grandmothers who often looked after the young ones while the parents were at work.

In preparation for the return to school parties, the discarded patches of back green land were treated by the young men as a challenge. They transformed their respective territories into clean, smart, open spaces. Retrieved from the air-raid shelters were the long timber benches that were then decorated with white tablecloths by the women, who also provided food and refreshments for the kids. Huge kettles of tea and plenty of lemonade, along with ice cream and jelly, were laid on the tables for the young ones, all of which was ferociously consumed within minutes of being offered. But the parents made sure that there was plenty; different mothers provided their own specialities, which they presented with great pride to the devouring youngsters.

My mother's speciality was her famous clootie dumpling, which she faithfully made each year and which always proved to be one of the favourites. It's strange, but despite the unpredictability of Scottish weather, I can't remember any back green party that was ever spoiled by rain. The mind's eye is a strange thing, these parties always appeared to be held on warm, sunny days; perhaps I've simply chosen to omit the less memorable times.

These were pleasant times, when all neighbourhood rivalry was forgotten, at least for that day. People tended to be more content, with little personal rivalry between families. There was also an unspoken closeness between the generations. In such a cajoling atmosphere, any sour family relationships from the past were muffled and often, for the sake of the children, put right for good during such parties. Each family maintained their own privacy, but they also knew that neighbours were there if needed, even if only to keep a watchful eye on the youngsters before their parents returned from a day's work. Unfortunately, much of this unselfish social bond has since disappeared, perhaps gone forever, giving way to more materialistic and less sympathetic times.

These Were the Days

I will always remember our Friday nights when my parents treated themselves and me to an evening out at the movies, after which my father retreated into Cookie's, his local pub on the Hilltown, for a quick pint. My mother and I would then walk along Alexander Street. On the way, we always dropped into the local fish and chip shop, where I received two free fritters and my mother placed our usual order of two fish suppers, a single fish, and a bottle of Vimto, my favourite drink. The owner of the shop, Mrs Barbieri, and my mother would then chatter for what I thought was an age before we returned home. There, she set the table for the arrival of my father, who on his way collected the fish and chip order, which Mrs Barbieri had kept hot by wrapping everything well in newspaper. I always recognised his familiar footsteps climbing the three flights of tenement stairs; my mother would then quickly pour the tea for our supper together. My father and I ate the fish suppers while my mother had the fish. I then followed this up by drinking a large glass of Vimto.

We looked forward to these late Friday feasts, and as my father settled himself in front of the warm fire, my mother would bustle around tidying up. Although she liked to talk, on Friday evenings, it was my father who held centre stage. "Tell us about the old days, Dad," I would say to him. "Ah, they were the days," he would reply. "The young anes dinna ken their livn noo."[44] He would then lean back in his chair and in his old familiar entertaining voice recalled old times.

He would talk about when he was in the army during the First World War or as a fireman in the Second; occasionally, he would reminisce about his young life on the farm. In fact, during these Friday night sessions, he would talk about almost anything that came to mind, as if they were only yesterday. Eventually, we had heard all the Friday night stories, but he was so droll that I willingly listened to them again. This was my father at his best.

---

[44] "The young ones don't know they're living now."

To his array of stories, my mother of course contributed her memories, which often included the dance hall days or when she trained as a first aid worker during the war years. But it was my father's tales of the past that fascinated me most.

I clearly remember one story about his unit travelling through France during the 1914–18 war. They came across an orchard of apple trees that were right for picking, so they immediately started to help themselves to the fruit. During the war, when required, the soldiers would forage the land, giving a receipt for any food that was taken, which was then presented to the unit's headquarters by the farmer for reimbursement. However, this farmer was making a fuss, and of course, it was all in French, which nobody understood. After some hand waving and noisemaking, one of the unit's soldiers stepped forward; he came from Arbroath, a fishing village just seventeen miles east of Dundee. In his very distinct east coast accent, he took control of the situation. "It's OK, boys. I can speak the French." He then turned to the farmer, saluted, and in his best polite Arbroath drawl uttered, "We British soldiers. Div them aiples belang ti voo?"[45] Astonishingly, the farmer appeared to understand. "Ah Scotties," he declared with a smile spreading over his face. "Good luck, Scotties." He then shook the hands of the whole company and, with a receipt for the apples in his pocket, walked off. My father always maintained that the farmer had not a clue as to what the soldier had said, but he had recognised the Scottish accent, and as claimed by my father, "All foreigners like the Scots." I really believed that to be true. After all, my father had said it.

My mother would also recall her bygone youth, including the dancing days, starting work at 13, and how she met my dad. Some memories caused a tear to appear in her eyes, at which point my father would interrupt. "How aboot a nither cup o' tea, wife?"[46] At that point, my mother would rise and say, "Aye, wha's fir mare

---

[45] "We are British soldiers. Do these apples belong to you?"

[46] "How about another cup of tea, wife?"

tea?"[47] I could see that she was happy and content, which was unlike some wives, who dreaded and shook with fear at the thought of their husbands returning from the pub after their Friday night drinking session.

My folks were both lucky to have each other for such a long time, and I think I could speak for them both by saying that they loved each other deeply and that they had an extremely successful marriage.

Growing Up

Despite being a little pest at times to my aging parents—my father was in his sixties and my mother in her late fifties—we were a close family. While I was still attending secondary school, my brother Bill had graduated and left home. I, being a young teenager, had an attitude problem, which my father found no problem in dealing with. He would often threaten me with "a clout in the lug,"[48] and often that was no idle threat. No matter how much taller I had become in comparison to my father, this would put me back in my place, as I then dutifully respected his authority and wishes.

However, it was my mother who controlled us both, and it was her word that was law in the family. Also, she skilfully managed this remarkable feat by rarely raising her voice. My father and I rarely argued; when we did, it was normally good banter between us, but periodically we did have heated discussions about almost anything and everything.

During one such trivial deliberation involving a family photograph that had been enlarged and framed, my mother asked my father to hang the framed picture somewhere in the house. As to where and how in the house it should be hung became the contentious and heated issue. I remember remarking, "Dad if you ask me, the picture looks daft on that wall. Folk are going to laugh at it, and it's also squint." To

---

[47]   "Yes. Who's for more tea?"
[48]   "A smack on the side of the head."

my father, this was his task, not mine, so he cut my nose, retorting, "Well, son, I never asked you, and it's no squint, nor is it as daft as your haircut." This was a great insult to me, as I was extremely proud of my Tony Curtis hairstyle (Curtis was an American film star). My father continued his bombardment of words. "If you go oot lookin like that, a the lassies ul laugh at you, an' no ma picture."[49] At that, I checked my Tony hairstyle in the mirror and replied, "Dad, there's nothing wrang wi—" My father interrupted. "Ney mare o' yir cheek, yir no that big that yir father could'ni gee yi a clout in the lug."[50] He then paused before continuing. "An speakin aboot lassies, wh'is that lass ad seein yi wee the ither day?" Before I could answer, my mother came from the kitchen and was now standing in the hall examining the framed picture that was hanging at a slight angle. "That's nice, Dad," she said, smiling at us both. She always called him "Dad" when the family was around. I then stupidly clyped on my dad to my mum over his scurrilous remark about my haircut. "Dad said that my Tony looks daft." "Yes", was her quick reply, clearly agreeing with Dad. I was totally outgunned, and in a few seconds, we all looked at each other then, almost simultaneously, started to laugh. Through her infectious smile, she continued. "Yir like twa barns arguing, and jist as bad as aen another. Yir tea's ready noo, so bith o yi come an' sit doon."[51]

That was the extent of our family fallouts. Incidentally, I didn't dare suggest to my mother that the picture was squint.

---

[49] "If you go out looking like that, then the lassies will all laugh at you, and not my picture."

[50] "No more of your cheek. Yir no that big that yir father could'ni gee yi a clout in the lug."

[51] "You're like two kids arguing. You're just as bad as each other. Your tea is now ready, so both of you come and sit down."

A Late Child Is a Blessing, sometimes

I was a late child, perhaps even a mistake, appearing some twelve years after my brother (Bill). So, the age gap between us was such that we had little in common. I certainly do not recall him ever being there during those Friday evenings. But we had been brought up in the same environment by the same parents, and for years, we even shared the same bed. Hence, not only had we developed similar habits but also possessed many of the same innate traits. Unlike the rest of the family, we had a similar sense of humour; we loved the weekly radio broadcasts of the *Goon Show, Round the Horn,* and the weekly instalments of *Journey into Space,* to the utter bemusement of our father. We had the same craving for any kind of cheese. This was unique throughout the family. Also, I can't forget the irresistibly tasty clootie dumplings that my mother would regularly make, especially during Bill's national service years; I was only 7 years old at the time. Each fortnight, she would bake two dumplings, one of which was sent to Bill at his billet in Aldershot. The English soldiers referred to the dumpling as "Scotch cake," looking forward to its arrival and its sharing out; even the commanding officer expected a portion. The remaining dumpling was eaten mainly by me, who if allowed would have devoured it in its entirety.

Bill was a studious intellect from the previous decade, but I was not. I had a vein streak of a mischief-maker, which would appear in the most unexpected ways. I remember, at the age of 5, having started my primary school education and deciding that school life was not for me, so I simply stopped attending. Concealed in the long grass just opposite the school gate, I amused myself until lunch, whereupon I would return to Dallfield Walk, to my grandparents' house for a plate of soup and a pudding. The same procedure was then repeated in the afternoon, when I appeared for the evening meal, after which I would be collected by my mother after her work. This went on for a full week, but the next Monday morning, my absence was reported to my grandparents. I fully expected my father to deliver one of his hard clouts, but he didn't. He had done the same when he was my age and was severely punished for it, which made him dislike school and its discipline even more. I received a severe scolding from school and parents alike and was told that if this absconding habit continued, I would never learn to read or write. It seemed to work; never again did I shirk from my schooling. But the real reason that put an end to this truant behaviour was the look of disappointment on my mother's face, which I never forgot, and the accompanying feeling of shame felt. Despite this, I never did like the primary school; it was a drudge that ground on for seven long years. I remember being told by my primary six teacher, Miss Japp, that I was not as good as my brother. She had taught him eleven years before me, and the remark was probably true, but it stayed with me to this day, as did the disappointed look on my mother's face.

Nevertheless, there were other devilish activities that I wholeheartedly pursued during these infantile pre-teen years. I recall on several occasions charging through the side entrance of the Ellenbank bar (the local pub), accompanied by my sidekick and best friend, David Miles. We would reappear out through the saloon-styled swing doors at the front. As we ran across the sawdust-covered floor of the pub, we would shout at the top of our young voices, "Up with United!" which was (and still is) one of Dundee's local football teams. We both thought this to be a daring act of extreme courage as the Ellenbank pub, at least at that time, was mostly frequented by the opposing supports and acrimonious rivals to United, and that was (and still is) Dundee FC. We were never caught. In fact, I don't think that the hard-drinking occupants even noticed our act of intrusive valour.

Regardless of such bold deeds, and my father's fascination for football, I was never sufficiently interested in the game as to become actively involved or even show any inclination towards it. However, I do remember ducking under the bars of the payment booth at Tannadice (Dundee United's stadium). This was a trick which allowed youngsters into the football ground free of charge. A willing adult entering the booth would pay as normal, but as the bars opened to allow him in, he would allow a youngster to quickly duck below the payment hatch and into the stadium unobserved.

CHAPTER 14

Early Childhood

My Gang

At around the age of 9 or 10, I formed a small band of loyal cohorts and formed what we referred to as the Forky Gang. It consisted of three boys (the other two being my friends Davie and Jimmy, his brother, who lived two doors down on the same plat) plus two somewhat unwilling girls, who lived in the same tenement block and always just seemed to be there; these female recruits into this band of adventurers also increased its numbers. An added advantage of the girls was that one would call up to her mother for something to eat. The mother, being all too glad to see us playing together instead of fighting, would duly spread five slices of bread with jam, wrap them up in newspaper, and throw them over the plat into the back green, whereby each gang member received a "jammy piece." The gang was then ready to pursue and fulfil its prime objective, hence, its grand title. This was to seek out and destroy all forked-tailed creatures (Dundee vernacular for earwigs) from the planet. This purge and eradication of all earwigs was taken extremely seriously by all the gang members, to the extent that a declaration of war was declared prior to any engagement against these innocent creatures. Then, with sticks and stones, and great gusto, we attacked to eradicate these beasts. This, however, was soon brought to a decisive end when the gang was informed, in no uncertain terms, that the earwigs, far from being raze to oblivion, had escaped en masse and, despite our onslaught, taken up alternative residence in the nearby tenements, to the clamorous verbosities of the occupants.

Part of the Forky Gang. I'm to the right, David is to the left, and in the middle is one of the girls.

This was a setback but was not the end of the gang's planned activities. Huddled inside our air-raid shelter (our headquarters), the gang planned an even greater enterprise. This was the period during post-war Britain's recovery, when our vast allied armies had been victorious over evil. Such thoughts had been installed in our ripe young minds and inspired by the release of the all-action Hollywood blockbuster *Quo Vadis,* which was set against the ancient Roman

Empire and conquest. We likewise planned the conquest of a vast domain, which was to be quite sizable, consisting most of the local neighbourhood including its streets, pends, back greens, and air-raid shelters. It was intended to include part of Caldrum Street to the north, but that was already occupied by older and bigger boys, so the decision was made, after great deliberation, to be more prudent and observe the status quo by consolidating a somewhat lesser and more manageable realm. My mother had given me the inside lining of an old coat, which was the ideal colour, purple. Hence, as emperor and leader of the gang, I was paraded around our newly won territories while wearing the royal purple and a painted berry basket on my head for a crown, regally waving to passers-by, who would more than likely smile with amusement and wave back. Little did they know that they were now subjects of the Forky Gang.

This was not only great fun and part of growing up, but it also encapsulated our imagination, creating for ourselves simpler and more succinct memories of a less than perfect world. I often wonder where that mischievous little boy had gone; did he simply evaporate under seven decades of stressed adulthood, or is he still there, straining to be drawn out from the veneer of mellowing maturity? Even now, my infantile sense of humour appears to be a direct throwback to these early days. At heart, I think that immature child may still be there.

Self and Family

As I grew into a normal teenager, if there is any such thing, I passed through the normal phases of knowing everything (while indeed knowing almost nothing). As was the norm for any young teenager, I joined a newly formed rock group, as a drummer, knowing absolutely nothing about any percussion instrument and trusting that nobody would notice my somewhat limited drumming skills. This was not the case, as my deceitfulness was quickly noticed by my more musical colleagues. I was cast out of the band by my fellow musicians—a humiliating episode in my young life.

During this period of attempted fame, I was employed as a junior salesman in a local jewellery shop. This was my first job, and the only one that I was ever fired from, mainly for attitude. However, in the affluent suburb of Broughty Ferry, I did manage to secure employment, and there, in a family-run hardware store, I served my time as an ironmonger earning the grand total of £2.50 per week. This was not my idea of gainful employment, and I intensely disliked my working life, but at least it was a job. I will always remember regularly checking my watch as I wearisomely, but politely, served customers. It always seemed to be hours before my lunch break at twelve noon. During these laboriously long hours, I exercised my ironmongery skills by counting out woodscrews for agitated customers or filling empty shelves with dozens of bottles of turpentine, perhaps even lifting heavy creosote barrels onto shelves in the back store. In this, along with other equally tedious tasks, I occupied myself from eight thirty in the morning until six o'clock in the evening, before I could with mind-numbing relief close the front door of the shop and leave for home. I felt a captive in this monotonous shopkeeping job, so I left as soon as was possibly, some three years later.

This was self-inflicted torture, so I left to join the RAF. My intent was to follow a career in the forces, and that would have been the case but for the unfortunate discovery of a hernia during a routine medical examination. After the operation, and during my six-week convalescence, I found an even better job; this time with the National Cash Register Company (NCR), in Dundee. There, I was employed as a storeman but quickly became part of the production control team, probably due to my experience in stock control while an ironmonger. Hence, all had not been in vain.

During this time, in the sixties, I was married (1966) to the most beautiful girl I had ever seen. Now with a wife, I looked forward to the future. We had three daughters (Denise, Karen, and Laure), all of whom are now married with their own families. I currently have a total of six grandchildren and eight great-grandchildren. The age range between the oldest and youngest of my grandchildren spans more than twenty years.

As a student

While a stock controller with the Dundee branch of the NCR, I knew almost every phase in the production of mechanical cash registers. At one end of the factory, I would watch and logged in the thin sheets of steel that entered the raw material stores. Then following this sheet metal out onto the factory floor and through the various stages of subassemblies, I would check out the final and complete cash register machines that appeared at the other end of the production process. I was one of the few who had the privilege of watching the entire procedure, and it fascinated me as to how the human mind could think through and create such a useful multifaceted system, at the end of which was a useful machine of such complexity.

Nevertheless, being a stock controller, it was clear that due to lack of investment at the research stages, the company was falling behind its market rivals. I always remember asking at a seminar why the company had researched its new computer (the Computronic machine) using the denary counting system (base ten) whereas our competitors were overtaking us by using the more efficient binary system (base two), which was cheaper and better. Also, by looking ahead at incoming orders, it was clear that we were depending on follow-up business and that very few new orders were being logged. After four good years of work with this manufacturing firm, I decided that a change was necessary, and with the support of my wife, I started to earnestly study, entering Dundee University at the age of almost 30. This was an attempt to firmly secure the family's eventual future in a still uncertain world.

On completion of each set of term exams followed a break from studies. These were the short Christmas and Easter holidays, followed by the three-month summer vacation. As I was a matured married student with three of a family, it was imperative that I found employment as soon as the exams were over, which meant I would work anywhere, thus supplementing my meagre grant.

One of the better venues of employment was as an assistant care worker in the council-owned retirement home in the city (the Rowans). The building had been the city's East Poor House during Victorian times. Built in 1856 by the Parochial Board of Dundee, it was partitioned into infirmed and elderly sections; normally attached to such buildings was a smaller section, which was literally referred to as the lunatic asylum, this being the forerunner of the present-day psychiatric hospital. I was employed in the Rowans at the latter end of the 1960s. The building had been much changed from the previous century; however, it could still easily be recognised by its then bell-less belfry, sitting aloft, which was a throwback to a less charitable era. Due to the Rowan's reputation as the old poorhouse, it was regarded as a place where one would not want to be at the end of their days. It was talked about with some fear and trepidation, particularly among the elderly, many of whom could remember such early days. One of the more unusual residents was that of a hen. It was free to wander the grounds of the Rowans, laying the odd egg as it went. It was named Pricilla and was a great pet and favourite among the old folk and staff, who were greeted each morning by its clucking as the early shift entered through the front gate. The Rowan's chef often threatened that if there had been enough eating on it, he would have put it into the pot.

As an employee, I must say that working among these old people, of which I am now one, was the most satisfying of all my lifelong working experiences. And that included my forty years as a teacher; it profoundly changed the way I viewed the world and helped me prepare for my future life as a senior citizen; it was one of my inspirations for writing this book.

If this first choice of employment was not available at the start of the summer term, then a less salubrious job was in the local Smedley's canning and fruit factory. Here, the work was relatively easy and straightforward but laborious and tedious. Nevertheless, with long, working shifts, the money was good.

My second inspiration for writing this book was a place where, like the Rowans, no one really wanted to be, the Dundee jute mills.

During the long, drudge-filled summer breaks, I worked as an Airton spool winder or cop winder in almost every jute mill that remained in the city. I preferred the nightshift as it had a higher rate of pay; also, it was easier to find work as a night worker. Only men did the nightshift, a few having been placed there by the police to keep them out of mischief or harm's way.

It was not unusual to find local students working in these Dundee mills. The work was relatively easy to learn. (After all those years, I can still tie the weaver's knot.) The problem was endurance and the monotony of continuous repetitive work; also, the noise of the clattering machinery that had to be operated in tropical heat and humid conditions needed to keep the yarn pliable. Another factor was the dust. It lingered in the air like a thick floating mist, getting everywhere including one's lungs. After a fortnight in a mill, I was always extremely sick. This was known as jute fever and was the accumulation of fibres in the gut. The sickness lasted only a few days, after which one's immune system set in. Jute fever apparently disappears with no outward signs. The damage that was being done internally to long-term jute workers would only show later in life.

My First Jute Fire

It was in the Angus Jute Factory in Dundee's Isla Street, during my second night of employment. I noticed smoke at the far end of my jute frame, some twenty yards away. There was a sudden flash of bright-orange light followed by numerous individual lines of small advancing fireballs that twisted and snaked their way through my frame at an astonishing speed. These individual balls of fire followed the line of the yarn, burning it to ash as it moved around the many attached guide and tension wheels. The entire process appeared to be synchronised as the fire rushed down the full length of the machine. As the yarn ignited, it was burnt to ash and smouldering embers, which in turn fell into the frame, setting it and the floor dust alight. Within a split second, the whole length of my machine was engulfed in a single ball of flame. Then the thick dust contained in the surrounding air also caught fire as I became part of the inferno. My initial feeling was of stunned shock as I stood in the centre of a furnace; there was no time for panic as the airburst flash had died down and disappeared as quickly as it had appeared. The thick hairs on my arms and eyebrows had been singed off, which left a strong smell of charred burning.

The real danger, however, was yet to come. Dust, saturated with machine oil that had accumulated on the underside of the frame, had been ignited, and this was by far a more ferocious fire. As word spread throughout the flat, men immediately ran to the burning machine with fire buckets that had been placed strategically throughout the factory. This appeared to be the only form of equipment or arrangement for the fighting of a jute fire; however, the routine appeared to be well-rehearsed, which was vital as there was only a narrow time gap during which the fire had to be contained and extinguished before the necessity of evacuating the flat.

We battled the inferno for what seemed to be an eternity until it was finally extinguished. Thick, black smoke then gushed from every part of my frame, bellowing towards the roof. The whole flat was engulfed in a dense blanket of darkness. It was only then that the windows were opened for ventilation. We, on this occasion, were lucky the fire was out, and after a short tea break, the whole flat went back to its normal routine. My frame, after a quick overhaul and clean, was surprisingly undamaged, and with the help of the gaffer, the machine with new yarn was rethreaded and restarted. The gaffer then turned to me and said, "Well, you've been in your first jute fire. It'll not be your last." He was right. I did experience more jute fires in the mills, but the first is always the most memorable. The nightshift then continued as if nothing extraordinary had happened. All was normal, except for the lingering stench of burnt oil and jute that persistently hung in the air and on one's clothes.

CHAPTER 15

Still Together

The End of the Old Days

R ecovery started in the early 1950s, when work and spare money became available. Also, there was a change in society and social thinking. The country had been introduced to the concept of hire purchase (HP), which meant that modern household contraptions were now available to ordinary working families. They included washing machines, radiograms, and of course, the television set. All bought on HP, which was often termed "the never-never" as each family would simply purchase their next item as soon as the previous one had been paid for.

The older generation often missed out, as they could not afford the luxuries that were now on offer. I remember Mr and Mrs Cowie, who were an old couple living at the opposite end of the landing, in Alexander Street. They had come to my parents' door for some reason and were invited in. The television had been switched on for the five o'clock *Children's Hour*. She had never seen a television before so was invited to sit down and watch this new phenomenon. She was taken aback. "Oh my. Look at that. I'll hey ti get Willie" was her reaction. Mrs Cowie dashed out of the door to fetch her husband, Willie.

Minutes later back she came with him in tow. She was a reserved and respectable person, and it was only then that she realised the family were all at their tea. "I'm sorry, Mrs Pullar. Yir at yir tea. What was I thinking aboot?"[52] she said, trying hastily to leave. "Never mind that. Come on in an' mak' yirsel at hame"[53] was the answer. They sat there for a large portion of the evening, supplied with tea and biscuits, until the closedown at ten o'clock and the national anthem was finally played. We were by no means the first to have such luxuries. That honour went to a family along the plat. I always had a certain amount of sympathy for them as at five o'clock sharp, the whole tenement block went silent, bereft of any children's voices. We could all be found crushed into Mr and Mrs Boyle's house, watching *Children's Hour*. This included the quiet watching of the fifteen-minute interlude when only a swimming goldfish or a silent waterfall was on display.

The prime minister of the day, Harold MacMillan, said, "You've never had it so good." Maybe so, but that was when the "old days" ended. The 1950s was the main period of change, when materialism started to influence everyday life. The Dundee mills were starting their final death knell descent; young families had started to move out, becoming aware of the wider world. Between 1945 and 1972, the assisted £10 passage, financed by the Australian government, attracted 1 million immigrants, many of whom were highly skilled to the shores of an expanding continent at the other side of the world. There were similar losses to other countries, which Britain could not afford; this included the brain drain of graduates and professional people to the United States of America.

Nonetheless, an affluent middle-class society started to appear, with their motor cars and family gadgetry. Also, year by year, there seemed to be many more motor cars congesting our roads. More fashionable furniture was being bought for homes, much of which

---

52 "I'm sorry, Mrs Pullar. You are all at your tea. What was I thinking?"
53 "Never mind that. Come in and make yourself at home."

was imported from Scandinavia (G-Plan had arrived). This apparent prosperity was credit generated and that was fine—for some.

The youth of the country had also started to follow their own fashions, influenced particularly by ideas imported from the United States. Music had become rock and roll, and food was the hamburger. However, clothes reflected a more homegrown style. The British-innovated Teddy Boy (and Girl) appeared on the scene. I of course, who was part of that generation, had to be different, so I became a self-proclaimed Vicky Boy. I had a magnificent dark-blue jacket that reached almost to my knees and was fitted out with a black, velvet lapel and collar. The rest of my outfit consisted of tight, black trousers referred to as "drainpipes," an extremely thin red tie called a "Slim Jim," and black, thick, crepe-sole shoes. Along with my Tony haircut, which was combed into a DA or "duck's ass" along with a neckline at the back, I must have been a sight worth seeing. My father just laughed and shook his head. He understood that this was a teenage phase and would soon disappear. He then explained how, in his youth, all the young men wore bell-bottomed, flared trousers. He would then add as a little good-humoured dig, "Ah wisni as daft lookin as you are in that outfit."[54] He would then laugh and turn back to reading his newspaper.

However, my mother could not look at me when dressed in my dress-code outfit for the dancing; she simply turned away each time this apparition appeared. "It's aboot tim he grew up," she would whisper to my father, and of course in time I did. I never knew what happened to these splendid pieces of attire. I once had a photograph of myself in full outfit, but it mysteriously disappeared along with my Vicky Boy suit. Perhaps my mother had something to do with that.

During this apparent period of progress, family structure started to change, and not for the better. No longer did people wish for what they needed. Instead, they became obsessed by what they wanted. Families became more reclusive and inward looking, visiting fewer friends and relatives. They chose instead to settle down and watch

---

[54] "I'm not as daft looking as you are in that outfit."

television. My brother and I were lucky as we had been encouraged to be outgoing; I preferred sports (swimming and cycling), and my brother, William, preferred hillwalking and reading. However, in some homes, conversation and interactions between siblings and parents almost stopped, and family activities, games, stories, songs, and reading were no more. For such families, an evening's entertainment consisted of sitting and watching "the box." Meals were no longer served and eaten round the family table, where conversations were held, plans were made, and differences were settled; instead, food was consumed on one's lap, and again in silence except for the odd comment or outburst of laughter as all eyes were fixed on the screen. There was only one channel, which meant that at any one time almost the entire country could have been filtering the same set of thoughts through their rapidly diminishing android mine.

To reinforce this dilemma, vast council housing estates were rapidly being built on the outskirts of the city. The intent was good: to alleviate the overcrowded and slum conditions that many were living in. These new homes were essential to cope with the ever-increasing numbers of young children, known as the baby boom period, when demobbed soldiers at last came home. Such housing estates surrounded Dundee in a cocoon of brick and mortar, but they offered the occupants a new way of life that was clean and healthy, with plenty of fresh air and space to move away from the dust and grime of the city.

Most families benefited by their move to a modern home and enjoyed the freedom. They were popular with young families, where more than adequate accommodation was provided. However, adequate accommodation and fresh air did not compensate for the loss of the greater family circle, and that included the grandparents, brothers, sisters, aunts, uncles, and cousins, all in some way broken— in some cases forever. In the past, it was not unusual for such families to live all within a few streets of each other, but this was no longer the case. Council estates presented a completely new way of life that in some way affected us all. Due to the loss of often much-needed family contact and support, many families started to disintegrate. The young no longer followed the genuine guidance of a close relative. And a bolder stance began to creep into their language, whereby "I want" replaced "Can I have?" which was alien to the more mature advice offered from experienced and the more caring parents. The youth in the large city estates were not all to blame; they followed the patterns and standards that had been initially set by the parents, and they were the ones who controlled families, councils, and even government. The young ones within most cities (including Dundee) had been allowed to become driven by peer group pressure, which in turn produced a long-lasting defective legacy within the community. The result for some was a breakdown in communication and therefore much family distress.

The new modern family lifestyle was more acquisition based, where materialism was the all-important driving force. As a result, most social institutes declined; youth groups run by the council and churches almost disappeared; church attendances plummeted. Some good people tried to revive such activities, but it was never the same. They were secondary in importance and associated with the previous generation. In other words, they were no longer "cool." Parents and grandparents had simply become the old ones whose opinions and advice counted for nothing. Attitudes had changed, and in general, this applied not only to family members but to all urban society.

Reinforcing this social decline was the immense size of the Dundee housing estates. This frustrated law enforcement as the beat policeman no longer could cover such sprawled-out areas on foot; patrol cars became necessary, which lost much of the personal touch of the local beat bobby. Adolescent groups during my youth respected the local beat policemen. And despite an occasional chastisement from him, there was an element of trust whereby he was regarded more as a friend and certainly not an enemy. Often, the local bobbies would drop a hint indicating that they knew what mischief we intended to be up to that day. "Stop your run'in through the Ellenbank bar, shouting up with United." Then he would add, "Ye ken fine I'm a Dundee supporter."[55] Also, there was the unavoidable telling-off about attacking earwigs' nests, "Stop chasin' them forky tailies, they're a goi'n inti the low doon doors, and the tenants are kickin' up a row."[56]

My father often remarked that he was glad to have been born when he was, despite the two world wars, the idleness, and the hardship. He said that in his days they were poor, but they were all poor together, all in the same boat at the same time, and hence in their own way they were closer and happier.

In a similar way, I feel sorry for the young ones today. We had alcohol-free dancing every weekend in the J.M. Ballroom and the Palais, with cheap bus transport provided by the local authorities to see us home at the end of the evening. Every Tuesday evening was record night in the Emprise Ballroom (better known as the "Tonk" by the local youth). There, current records were played to an enthusiastic audience. During weekdays, there were the popular youth clubs where different activities were offered, including table tennis, badminton, football, even boxing, or just meeting one's friends in a friendly environment; however, at the end of the evening (nine o'clock), there were always music and dancing. Such venues almost ran themselves; adult supervision was only in the background organising the event and keeping the peace. During the summer months, groups of teenagers would bus down to the local seaside venues of Broughty Ferry or Arbroath, where we could not only dance in the Marine Ball Room but also enjoy the beach. Arbroath had an open-air swimming pool, which was an additional bonus. However, it was the dance halls that I preferred. Here, the boys would stroll around the sides of the dance floor, eyeing up the girls, who were apparently dancing in the centre of the ballroom but were in turn also eyeing up the boys. Today there are few such places for the 13- to 17-year-old teenage groups; they

---

[55] "Stop running through the Ellenbank Bar, shouting up with United. You know fine I'm a Dundee supporter."

[56] "Stop chasing those earwigs. They're going into the lower flats, and the occupants are complaining."

can only wander the streets, with their mobile phones, while the older ones hang around street corners until they are old enough to enter pubs (at 18 years old) and drink. Whose fault is that? What a prospect for the well-being of our youth; I'm glad I'm the age I am.

Perhaps one of Dundee's prime assets, the Dundee Law, could be utilised. Its potential is considerable, from artificial ski and skateboarding on its slopes to nature walks and everything in between.

Finally

For the family, things did turn out favourably in the long run. Both sons graduated with good degrees; they were the first in the family to do so, which was most satisfying for my proud parents. During my parents' married life, they always sought something better, treating life as a challenge and an adventure. They had their chances in life, but like so many working people of the time, they were both unwilling to take that jump and the responsibility that went with it. Although my mother was the more confident and enterprising, she was only prepared to work with her husband. But working for a boss, although often hard and disagreeable, was all my father knew; it was familiar. Taking on responsibilities or—even worse—working for themselves, with the fear of losing what little they had, was too much. He simply couldn't do it. However, they seemed to get a kick out of just living and waiting to see what would turn up next. They said that they had no complaints and always faced the future with confidence.

Dad, who had worked so hard for his family, passed away, 11 January 1982. He was aged 82, the ninth son and last of the Hilltown Pullars.

My parents in their late seventies on holiday, Largs, Scotland.

The Hilltown family of Pullars has all gone. It is only I (Young Sandy) who is left, but I will ensure that their *memory stays.*

I once asked my mother if she would have changed anything in her life. She gave me one of her beautiful smiles and said, "I had a fine man, and we had two fine sons, who gave us five granddaughters. They have all graduated and are doing well. I've changed what I could change, and things are just fine the way they are. I think I can see things out now."

After a short illness, my mother died peacefully on 4 August 2000 at the age of 96. She was the last of the McElroy family from Dallfield Walk.

Bessie at the age of 96 years.

Sandy with three of his grandchildren (Denise, Karen and Laura).

Epilogue

My mother, Bessie, and father Sandy were lights in the lives of all who knew them. Those lights have now gone, but the memory stays—and in such detail. The whole family miss them deeply and we shall never forget.

Printed in Great Britain
by Amazon